The Golf Manual

The Golf Manual
ALEX HAY

Foreword by Michael Bonallack
Chairman of The Golf Foundation

Faber & Faber

Created by The Wordsmiths
Company Limited
Park House
Old Wolverton Road
Wolverton
Milton Keynes MK12 5QB
England

First published by Faber and
Faber Limited
3 Queen Square
London WC1N 3AU

ISBN 0 571 11642 6

The creators and publishers
acknowledge:
Kay Williams: editing
Sixpenny Studios: graphics
formulation
Frank Taylor: illustration and
design
Ian M Kerr: conceptualization

Typeset by Definition
Reprographics Ltd
Printed in Great Britain by
Powage Press

*Alex Hay with Harry Carpenter just
prior to 'going on the air' at Wentworth.*

CONTENTS

Foreword

FOREWORD

The Golf Foundation, as promoters of golf for young people, is always being asked for advice from would-be golfers, of all ages, as to how to get started in the game.

In this book Alex Hay has not only answered the various questions usually posed by a beginner but then goes to considerable length to describe in detail, with the help of some excellent drawings, not only the fundamentals of the game but also to give some excellent advice to the better golfer on how to face up to the more unusual shots — thereby serving both strokes and patience.

The first part of the book deals with the equipment required to play golf at various levels. A good deal of nonsense is talked about characteristics of shafts, clubs and balls, and most experienced players, let alone beginners, have no proper idea of which specification of club is best suited to their own physical make up but in this chapter (as in the rest of the book) sound advice is given which should enable even the newest of players to select the right equipment.

Having acquired the 'tools of the trade' we now turn to the fundamentals of grip, width of stance, ball position and posture, all of which are dealt with clearly and logically. In some ways this is the most important section of all, as only with the correct set-up and grip can all other aspects of the golf swing be allowed to function correctly. From here the pupil starts by learning the shorter shots first, and as his ability improves he slowly works his way back along the fairway, using the various clubs, until he finishes on the tee with the driver.

At first sight it might appear a complex book, but I am certain that if the reader takes his time and follows carefully the instructions and advice given in each chapter, he will soon realise that far from being complicated, he is actually being introduced to the game in a natural and logical sequence; and not only is he learning what he should do, but also he is able to understand what the results of certain actions will be.

Once the basic techniques are understood there follow some excellent chapters giving considerable food for thought to low handicap golfers, as well as assistance to the beginner. In describing the way to face up to and play some of the more difficult shots, the same common sense approach is used and will help take a great deal of mystery out of playing from odd stances or from 'impossible' lies in bunkers or the rough.

Of course, even the best players develop faults from time to time and it is usually only those with experience who are able to diagnose correctly the reason for any particular bad shot. In this book will be found a simple step by step method enabling any golfer to realise why his 'perfect' swing has produced such an unfortunate result, informing him of the actions he should take to correct the fault.

The concluding chapters delve into the problems of temperament and give further advice on joining a club and how to adapt your game to unusual conditions, very often a test of temperament as well as technique. Finally, having made scratch golfers of all his readers, Alex Hay tells how to go about becoming a professional.

To sum up, I would say that this is a book written by a man who has given a great deal of thought, not only to the problems facing a beginner, but also to the questions frequently asked by golfers of several years' experience. It should prove of great benefit to all.

Now I am off to the practice ground, to get rid of my slice with the help of my friend Alex Hay.

MICHAEL BONALLACK
Chairman
The Golf Foundation

PART ONE — INTRODUCTORY

CHAPTER 1 — INTRODUCTION

Links are strips of green turf found around Britain's shores and in abundance along the east coast of Scotland, which stretch between the beach and that land considered fit for agriculture. The only thing for which they were once thought suitable was the grazing of sheep, or perhaps a few geese. It was not until six or seven centuries ago that, thanks to the initiative of a few sports-minded shepherds (and, later, fisher-folk), the game of golf began.

The best of the links are to be found along the river estuaries: St. Andrews, at the mouth of the Eden; Gullane and Muirfield, on the south side of the Firth of Forth; and many other, lesser-known homes of the game. Indeed, at one time it was possible to golf almost all the way from Edinburgh to North Berwick, a distance of some 30 miles: from Leith links via Portobello, Fisherow, Musselburgh (venue of past open championships), Prestonpans, Port Seton, Longniddry, Kilspindie, Luffness, Gullane and Muirfield to North Berwick links. The sandy turf was, and indeed still is, the finest soil for golf and fortunately good for very little else; so it is likely that links golf will be preserved for quite some time to come.

Because the links are so inextricable a part of golf's history, the British Open Championship is competed for annually on a circuit of exclusive British links which includes St. Andrews, Muirfield, Carnoustie, Royal Troon and Prestwick in Scotland; and Royal Lytham and St. Annes, Royal Birkdale, Hoylake and Royal St. Georges in England. This tradition will remain, even though golf's spreading tentacles moved inland many centuries ago and produced great inland courses.

It is understandable, then, that the design characteristics of the 'man-made' golf courses

13

throughout the world are based on the natural hazards encountered by the early golfers. Even the modern golf club derives from implements carved and hammered out centuries ago. Where the side of a sand dune collapsed, with the turf falling away to expose the sand, this gave the perfect design for a bunker. The gulleys and creeks that wound their way from the mainland out to sea are constructed now as water hazards. The famous water holes featured in golf courses designed by the renowned American designer Trent Jones are similar to many British links courses when the high spring tides have risen and flooded the fairway. The roads and tracks 'in play' on many modern championship courses owe their origins to the 17th at St. Andrews — the Road Hole, traditional wrecker of good scores; and also to the famous footpath across the 18th called Granny Clark's Wynd, where no doubt an elderly fishwife carried her creel from beach to town and eventually wore a track.

The game of golf in early days had to be played in the form of match play, with the winner he (or she — Mary Queen of Scots was a golfer!) who won the most holes. There would have been very little hope of completing all the holes: the hazards then to be encountered included cart ruts, hoof prints, gulleys, stone dykes and fisherman's nets laid out to dry. Other 'natural' hazards were provided by market stalls — and in those days, the ball had to be played where it lay. If several hacks failed to extricate it, then the hole was conceded and the players made their way to the next hole — the winner jubilant, the other examining the head of his club which would no doubt need re-shaping!

Today's golfers are protected by all sorts of rules which permit them to pick up the ball and remove it to a place where it may be successfully hit. Sometimes, in the case of a cart-rut, an animal scrape or for several other reasons, the lift can be free of penalty. Even on occasions where a penalty is incurred, the player may continue and complete the hole; and this has made the modern form of stroke-play golf — with major events over four rounds, 72 holes — the common practice. All championship courses are now of 18 holes whereas, in ancient times, the course was as many holes as the strip of linksland could afford.

Soon after the game originated, there arose an industry consisting of men who specialised in making clubs and balls. Families became renowned as clubmakers all along the east coast of Scotland and many of their names live on today. Very early clubs had lead or iron heads on wooden shafts; these were designed to remove balls from places never encountered by today's sophisticated players. Many of the shapes dreamed up are now to be found only in museums, for there is today a very strict control on the specification of all clubs: designs must be submitted to golf's ruling body, based at St. Andrews and called the Royal and Ancient Club.

With the coming of a 'feathery' ball — a skin, handstitched and stuffed with feathers — wooden-headed clubs were added to the range and the game took on a new shape, for now the ball could be swept off as well as punched. Shafts were lengthened and the angle at which the head 'came off' the shaft was flatter, so much longer distances could be covered.

As the utensils progressed and the courses improved, and rules were established to eliminate the need for 'unnatural' strokes,

the golf swing was evolving towards its present orthodox shape. This evolution is an ongoing thing — indeed, there have been radical swing changes over the last half-century — and will no doubt continue as science produces new materials and club modifications. However, this book is designed to show the golf swing as it is used today, not only by the best players in the world but by good club golfers who prove that, while they may have many individual characteristics, there are many parts of the swing which are accepted as 'musts'. For a player to enjoy the game, a basic knowledge of golf is essential; and the information in the following pages is designed to help, be you novice or expert, young or old, male or female.

The golf swing is made up of many moving parts, all of which must be understood and 'trained' so that when brought together as the complete *swing*, they contribute to and enhance the movement being made. This book will show how all the strokes are played and how a golfer may build, through a simple process, a swing capable of producing the correct strokes regularly.

One aspect of golf that tends to frighten off the beginner is the multiplicity of clubs. He sees 14 clubs — and believes there must be that many swing to be learned.

There is but one swing! The modifications to be made so that the one swing may be used on the different clubs are greatly determined by the club itself. The clubs which are intended to send the ball the furthest each have a long shaft, with a decreasing amount of angle on the clubface and a flatter lie. The player is thus able to stand tall and reach out, and the resulting greater freedom of movement permits a fuller swing.

As the club shaft reduces in length, the face of the club increases in loft (its ability to lift the ball) and the lie is more upright. This brings the player closer and more over the ball, so reducing the fullness of the arc, and at the same time forcing a more upright angle of attack.

The positioning of the ball is moved *forward* to encourage the sweep of the longer strokes and *back* to promote the punch of the short, steeper arc.

Between these two extremes lies a swing which, combined with appropriate ball position, may be thought of as 'one swing'. This book will show in words and diagrams how the beginner would develop from a small lofting stroke up to a full-blooded drive, though using the same muscles and the same sense of balance in both strokes. And it will show the experienced golfer how, when he has lost form, to search out the fault quickly and in the correct order, eliminate it properly and return to form.

To a swing built on the sound formula given, variations can be applied in order that 'manufactured' strokes may be played. These are an essential part of the 'vocabulary' necessary for a player to improve: recovery strokes, strokes from hillsides, strokes that must climb quickly, others that must fly low, strokes that will run on, others that will stop almost instantly on landing. All of these require variations from the theme — and that theme is a sound orthodox platform of swing, from which the player may stray yet to which he may safely return.

There is a time when the player must accept a moderate result and not be foolishly adventurous; and there is a time when the opposite might apply. The importance of that 'when' is demonstrated here; and the strategy and psychology of golf dealt with also.

Etiquette, which covers the good manners and consideration recognised as an integral part of this great game, is explained to enable a player to enjoy golf and to allow fellow golfers to do the same.

The system of how golf clubs operate and how handicaps are allocated is also covered. In fact, the reader may travel through from novice to tournament professional and understand fully how to go about getting from one to another, should that be his or her desire. On the other hand, if the purpose of reading is simply to improve, these pages will certainly help.

There is an expression in golf: 'You drive for show, and you putt for dough!' Nancy Lopez, greatest lady golfer of all time, tees off with an iron — then gets down to business.
(Ken Lewis/Peter Dazeley)

CHAPTER 2 — EQUIPMENT

Anyone wishing to spend a fortune would make a wise choice by taking up golf, for there are sufficient accessories and pieces of equipment available to absorb rapidly a great deal of wealth! At the other end of the scale, however, it is possible to play good golf — with absolutely no feeling of inadequacy and with no disadvantage — on the most meagre of investments. The aim here is to explain exactly what is needed, from the very minimum requirements: to show which equipment is essential to the player's proper development and progress; what should be looked for and what should be avoided — for while good clubs do not necessarily make a good player, the wrong clubs will certainly prevent you becoming one. (Accessories — the host of bits and pieces increasingly available — are not dealt with here. As the word implies, they are non-essentials.)

CHAPTER 3 — THE CLUBS

Before 'matched sets', with swing-weights, shaft flexes, varying grip thicknesses and so on, were available, clubs were known by name rather than by number. With the limited amount of names, and players demanding more clubs, however, the numbering system began. At one time, just prior to the limiting of a set to the maximum of 14, many golfers were filling their bags with all sorts of clubs in an effort to have one for every shot they might encounter. One American professional who came over to Britain in the 1930s required two caddies to carry his clubs! In all, he had about 30 different varieties, which the caddies transported about the course in two bags.

The early clubs, which lasted until the numbering system took over, were called:

DRIVER

This, though still known as the driver, is the modern no. 1 wood.

It had very little loft on the face, often showing no more than four or five degrees. It was favoured for low shots into the wind but was extremely difficult to use.

Today's no. 1 wood shows a face loft of 12 degrees, which makes it much simpler to use.

BRASSIE

This is now called the no. 2 wood, but is gradually losing its place in sets of clubs. The reason for this is that it was used by many players who could not get the ball in the air with the poor angle of clubface on early drivers. Now that the modern driver is easier there is no need for the 2 wood from the tee — it is a very difficult club for average players to get the ball up off the grass.

It was always made with a heavy brass plate on its base to help it swing through under the ball, hence the name.

SPOON

Now called the no. 3 wood. A good club for hitting long shots from the fairways.

The modern version has an angled face of 16 degrees and is the favourite fairway wood for most players.

BAFFIE

This was today's no. 4 and 5 woods. The very shallow heads, and loft of 20 to 25 degrees, combined with a heavier swingweight makes them easy to use. They elevate the ball quickly, and are ideal for shots from moderate lies in rough grass.

DRIVING IRON

Now a no. 1 or no. 2 iron and often used (particularly the no. 1) by professionals who would rather be safely straight, if short, on a particularly dangerous tee shot; in short, who favour accuracy over distance.

Beginner golfers would be well advised to stay clear of using either of these clubs, for the low degree of loft face (14 on a 1, 18 on the 2) requires a swing of advanced skill.

LONG IRON

The no. 3 and no. 4 iron have taken the place of this club. They are used to hit the fairway strokes to the green when the ball lies at the appropriate yardage from the green.

MASHIE

Would be today's no. 5 iron (30 degrees) or no. 6 iron (34 degrees).

Ideal clubs not only for their appropriate distance, but from semi-rough lies off the fairway.

MASHIE NIBLICK

No. 7 (38 degrees) and no. 8 (42 degrees) irons would take this one's place.

Both are easy clubs with which to get good loft and yet good yardage.

NIBLICK

Once the most lofted club, used to get the ball up quickly, whether over trouble or simply out of it.

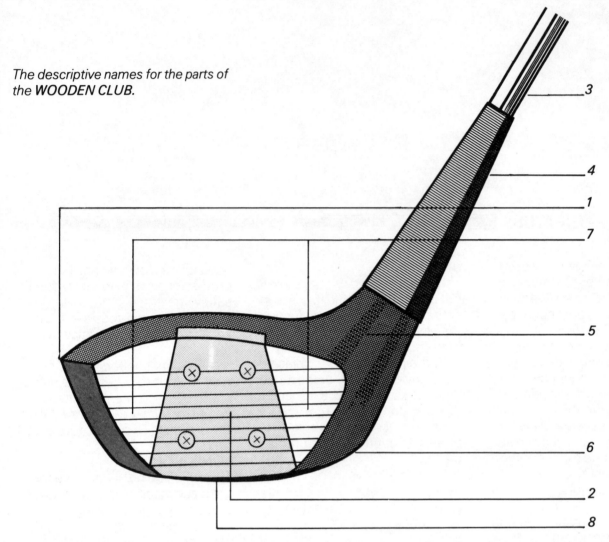

The descriptive names for the parts of the **WOODEN CLUB**.

1 **TOE** Sometimes described as the nose but toe is correct.

2 **INSERT** Normally made from a very hard plastic, but occasionally from metal.

3 **SHAFT** The head is bored so that the shaft passes right through and out of the bottom where it is cut off.

4 **NECK BINDING** This should be replaced regularly and a club should never be used if it is missing.

5 **NECK** The wood is tapered to paper thickness accuracy and must be protected by a secure binding.

6 **HEEL** A ball hit from this end of the club sends an 'echo' right up the shaft, which stings the fingers.

7 **FACE** The grooves in the face are a regulation width apart and they should be kept free of dirt as they are an aid to backspin.

8 **SOLE** The sole is protected by a metal plate secured by four screws. Often, under this plate, is sunk the lead weighting of the club. The plate is often aluminium in the case of a driver, yet brass with the no. 3, 4 and 5 woods. The reason for this is that as the shaft length increases the swinging weight of the club increases, so the long driver must carry the lightest plate in order to match the others in the set.

The individual parts of an *IRON CLUB* head (often called the blade).

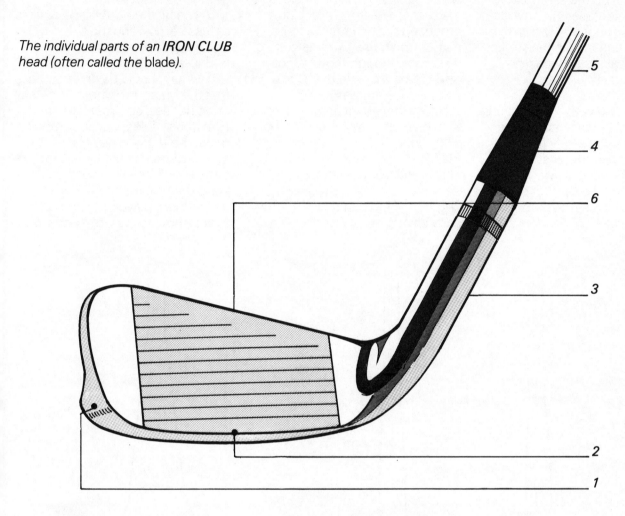

1. *TOE* A ball struck from here will cause the grip to be loosened.
2. *LEADING EDGE* This must be set accurately square before the grip is taken up.

3. *SOCKET* When the arc travels too much from inside to out this may contact the ball and send it at right angles, to the right.
4. *FERRULE* The plastic joint originally used to blend the shaft and the head to keep water from rusting the shaft at that point.

5. *SHAFT* The shaft is sunk into the head for approximately two thirds of the socket length and, though it used to be secured by a rivet, is now held by its tight fit plus modern adhesives.

Today the no. 9 iron and pitching wedge (46 and 52 degrees respectively) do the same job.

In addition, we now have a sand iron (58 degrees), which has a heavy sole and makes the strokes from the bunkers a much more simple affair.

JIGGER

This was a club with a short handle but with the loft of a modern no. 4 iron. It was used solely from the fringes of the green; just that awkward distance at which the player cannot use a putter because of the thicker grass, but is too close to pitch the ball.

Today the shot is called a run-up and may often be played by adapting one of the other clubs in the set. There are similar clubs produced today under various names and many average golfers use them, though they are not often to be found in the bags of the competitive professionals who would rather adapt another club than give up one of their 14 allocation.

PUTTER

This is still a putter; though the early model often had a few degrees of loft on its face. In the early days greens were cut in a primitive fashion by today's standards, and the loft helped to get the ball moving.

Today, the putter face is more or less vertical and the ball encouraged to roll rather than bounce.

What should be understood is that the fitting-in of more clubs was done not as a commercial venture, to increase sales; but as an effort to minimise the 'journey gap' — the gap between the distances the different clubs in the set would send the ball. In the case of a tournament player, he will know exactly how far he hits the ball with

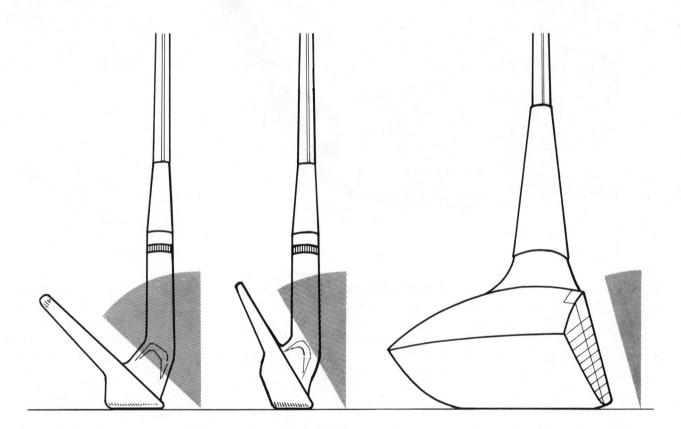

A. The **PITCHING WEDGE** is set at 52 degrees.

B. The no. **6 IRON** is set at 34 degrees.

C. The **DRIVER** is set at 12 degrees.

The 'degree of loft' refers to the angle at which the clubface is set back from a vertical line.

Although there are always 4 degrees between each of the irons,

which represents about 10 to 12 yards, the tournament professional often has his irons set with a couple of degrees less than standard. This is not a case of vanity, whereby he can send the ball

farther than the amateur, but a means of driving the ball lower in flight.

Unlike the average player his problem is not 'getting it up' but rather 'keeping it down'.

every club in his set, the gap being about 10 yards per club. In this way he can select the right club for the yardage he has to cover. That is why spectators see player and caddy consulting charts they have made (many golf clubs supply their own yardage booklets), before selecting the club for the job.

This is a very important lesson to be learned; for even the most humble of golfers should know how far he sends a ball with each club. It is only a matter of hitting 20 or so balls up a practice ground and pacing out to the best of them. The *best* — for a player should always select the club in the hope of a good shot, never with the negative state of mind that a bad one might happen. Good golf and positivity go hand in glove!

The Set of Clubs

There are various computations for what makes up a full set of clubs. The professional golfer usually carries three wooden clubs. His first two are a driver, and one that is marked no. 3 but often de-lofted to be somewhere between a 2 and a 3. This club is very powerful: with it, he can hit the ball a long way from a fairway lie. His third wood is a lofted one, probably a 4, and this he uses both for elevated long shots and from semi-rough. Often, when on the fairway but with an awkward stance, it is safer to play the no. 4 than to play the 3; there is always safety in loft!

His irons are ten in number: a 1 or 2 iron (according to preference) then 3, 4, 5, 6, 7, 8, 9, a pitching wedge and a sand iron. This leaves the putter as his fourteenth. Professionals who prefer to include both the 1 and 2 irons leave out the 4 wood and carry only one fairway wood.

The standard set of 14 clubs sold to average club golfers allows for four wooden clubs and is made

up as 1, 3 and 4 plus a 5 wood — because (though most wouldn't admit it) playing wooden club shots is easier than long iron shots. The flat base of the wooden club gives the opportunity to slide into the ball when the player is perhaps a little inaccurate; whereas the sharp edge of an iron penetrates the turf immediately on contact and therefore allows little margin for error. The 1 and 2 irons are not supplied in the average set, which begins with the 3 and runs through the set to the sand iron plus the putter.

So much for the maximum amount of clubs. But what about the minimum — the number of clubs that would enable a beginner to get going in golf at the lowest cost yet without making it impossible to achieve progress? The answer to that question is *five*.

A single wooden club would suffice, one that could double up for the tee shots as well as the fairway shots; so a lofted face is essential. Ideal would be a 3 wood. A minimum of three irons is essential: a long iron (which could be either a 3 or a 4); next a middle iron (say a 6 or 7); for the short shots around the green and to double up for bunker shots, a very lofted club (either a 9 iron or a wedge); and finally a putter.

Such a selection is limiting, yet sufficient to allow a person to determine whether he or she has an aptitude for the game. This minimum combination of clubs is suitable for man, woman or child. Great care should be taken when choosing clubs for children, however — such clubs must be suitable for cutting down to size. This job is done by the club professional, who is the best person to advise on and supply clubs. When a golf club is made shorter, it causes the shaft to get stiffer and this is not desirable for a

weak-wristed child. Clubs that are relatively light and flexible in the shaft are therefore best for children. Fortunately, a golf shaft tapers, and when a piece is sawn from the top of the shaft the remainder is slimmer, allowing the handle to be thinner, which is necessary for the small hands of the child. Ladies' clubs, incidentally, are only a half-to-one-inch shorter than men's, but are made so that the shafts leave the heads at a flattened angle.

It is extremely difficult these days to build up a set by adding to it over a period of time. Models change frequently, and once old stocks are cleared that is the end of it. Sometimes it is necessary for a beginner to trade in his 'few' clubs when his progress warrants more. This is not a bad thing, for acquiring the new set in one go ensures that the new clubs, even if 'new' second-hand ones, will be matched in weight and length. The first sign of promotion is when a driver is required, for this means that the loft of the 3 wood is no longer necessary and is sending the ball too high from a tee peg.

Choosing Your Clubs

While the very first few clubs can safely be of doubtful design, it would be a mistake not to take design into account when the bigger set is acquired. At this stage, there are one or two factors which *must* be taken into account if the player is to benefit and not simply to waste time and money.

The lie

The feature in which accuracy is most important is the *lie* of the club. This is the angle at which the shaft comes from the head when the base of the club is resting on the turf. Should the lie be incorrect, the player will endeavour to suit his physique to the club — and that is putting the cart before the horse. It is essential that the tall person uses clubs whose angle is set upright; and that the small person has clubs with a flatter lie.

A tall player attempting to use a flat-lying club will find that the *toe-end* of the clubhead will contact the ground first, thereby driving the heel of the club forward and pushing the ball off-line to the right.

A shorter person using an upright club would find the heel-end contacting, making the toe of the clubhead twist in and turn the ball away to the left.

The player with the correct club has the club square against the turf when meeting the ball, and straight shots are therefore possible.

Fortunately, since most 'iron' clubs are made with fairly soft steel heads, it is possible for a skilled club professional to adjust a club by bending its neck to suit the golfer. Wooden clubs are more difficult to alter, but because of their long handles are not normally too far out.

The clubface

The lines grooved on the faces of golf clubs are of a specified depth and width apart. Lines too close and too deep have the effect of increasing the backspin put on the ball and this is judged to be unfair. Lines too shallow and too far apart would allow the ball to skid, particularly on a wet day.

It has often been said that lines — or grooves, as they are often called — make no difference at all; but so far no great player has chosen to use clubs which have none. Many years ago, on the eve of a Ryder Cup Match between the United States and Great Britain, the American team captain claimed that some of the British players were using clubs with grooves and

When a tall person attempts to use a club which has a flat lie the heel of the club will be off the turf when he lines up to the ball.

Should the toe catch the ground, even though it be only a fraction prior to impact with the ball, the blade will spin so that the face becomes open; the ball will fly off to the right.

It must also be realised that many tall people adjust their posture as a means of getting the sole of the club level with the turf. This is a definite way of deforming the golf swing. Clubs should always be made to suit the player, never the reverse.

A shorter golfer, using an upright club, will find that only the heel of the club rests on the turf, with the toe pointing up in the air.

Should the ground be contacted prior to contact with the ball — and this is extremely likely — the clubface will spin closed and the ball will be pulled away to the left.

It is common for the smaller player to arch his wrists as a way of getting the sole of the club level on the turf. Doing so immobilises the wrists so that there can be no feel in the shot.

The clubs must be designed to fit the player.

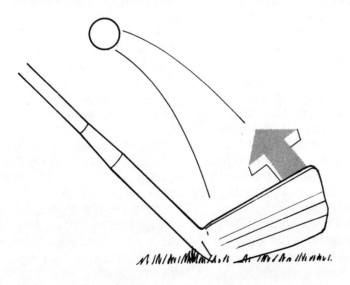

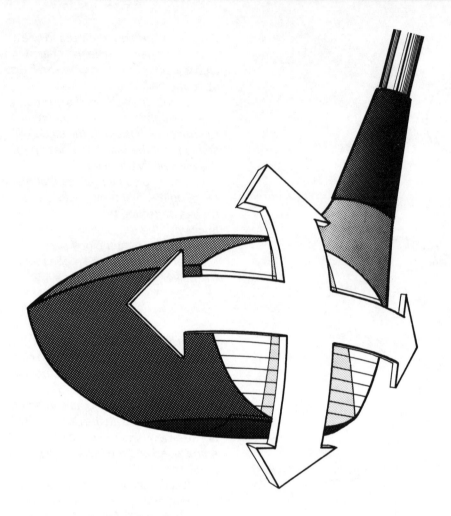

Many explanations have been given for the FOUR-WAY-ROLL which exists on the faces of all woods but is most defined on the driver.

One suggestion is that it stops the adhesion which is experienced on the level surface of an iron blade aiding backspin, for woods do not require so much spin.

Another comes from the fact that, when the bottom of the driver is examined, the scratch lines scored across the baseplate, plus the paint marks from tee pegs which have passed beneath the club, are never straight. In fact they travel diagonally across it and show the club head to be crossing the ball to target line from out-to-in. Therefore, were there no curve on the face the ball would be misdirected.

No one is really sure, though many ideas are offered; nevertheless all the clubmakers put it on, as the ball doesn't fly well without it.

drilled holes (which at one time served the same purpose as grooves) that were too deep. All the sets had to be re-ground to conform. That man, though unfortunate in his time, was right; for unfair advantage was being gained.

Players should always ensure that the grooves, which tend to fill with mud and dirt, are cleaned out regularly. This is one of the duties professional caddies attend to fastidiously.

Wooden clubfaces often have inserted into them a hard substance secured by either screws or glue. Occasionally the screwheads become proud and often, when the player neglects the clubs, the wooden parts of the face

swell above the level of the insert. This will certainly have the effect of sending the ball way off line. The woods should be checked and varnished regularly.

Four-Way Roll

While the face of the iron club is absolutely level, that of the wooden club is not. It is shaped into what is known as the 'four-way roll', which is a bulge curve from top to sole. This curve is essential to prevent adhesion of the ball to the surface; for the wood, unlike the iron, seeks not to create backspin but to minimise it. The face of the putter is without grooves and normally has no angle, being practically vertical.

The flex

Another priority factor is the shaft flex, of which there are four basic grades.

STIFF	(S)
REGULAR	(R)
A SHAFT	(A)
LADIES	(L)

A man with strong hands and supple wrists would find consistency only with the stiff shaft. Mr. Average would do well with the regular. Older golfers and stronger ladies would be best suited with the A shaft; while average ladies and children would do their best with the L shaft. Clubs cut down for the youngster should come from the A or L range, because to shorten is to stiffen (a point demonstrated by the nervous golfer who tries to protect himself by placing his hands down the grip — the stiffening effect makes him feel more secure).

The grip

The handles on second-hand clubs tend to be worn and shiny. If they are of the modern rubber variety, it is surprising what a good scrub in hot, soapy water will do to revive them. If they are too slippery, however, they must be replaced. This is done by the professional at any golf club — non-members are welcome to go and ask his advice; and repairs are often done at a surprisingly low cost. In addition to texture, the thickness of the handle is very important. Too thick a grip stifles free movement of the wrists, while a slim grip has exactly the opposite effect. The size of the player's hands must be the guide.

Choosing a putter

There is a vast range of putting implements available. The player should select one that feels well-balanced and sits with its base level on the turf. It is not true that any old thing will do for putting: every effort should be made to acquire a good putter.

Many professionals' shops have what is known as a 'sin bin', into which members who are sick of the sight of their putter (the psychological side of golf!) can throw the old one and, for a small charge, take out another. So it is possible to pay a visit to the pro shop and come out with a bargain!

Maintenance

A player should look after his golf clubs, for neglect is soon noticeable and leads to great expense.

Because the wooden club is vulnerable to damp, the whole club should be wiped dry after a round and stored in a dry place. Headcovers, which should be religiously replaced between strokes, should be stored separately when wet.

Irons should be wiped dry, particularly around where the shaft fits into the head — an area where moisture may cause rust and eventual fracture.

Once again, the club professional can help, with his maintenance service. Clubheads may be repolished and varnished; broken shafts replaced: grips fitted; in fact, he can do everything necessary, and offer a wealth of free good advice into the bargain.

CHAPTER 4 — OTHER EQUIPMENT

It is not necessary to deal with 'other equipment' at length here, because one acquires it over a period of time. Briefly, however, a golfer requires good spiked shoes, for good footwork and confidence in balance.

A carry-bag will suffice for part sets; only when a full set is acquired does the addition of a trolley become essential. (A small bag ruins the club handles when a full set is squeezed in.)

A glove is more a helpful luxury than a necessity, though there is no doubt that secure contact with the handle is assured when a glove is worn.

Provided a brand name is chosen, golf balls are all of a good standard. Moderately priced golf balls are certainly adequate for beginners. There are two sizes: 1.68'' (American Size) and 1.62'' (British Size). Both weigh 1.62 oz. While the big one seems the easier to hit, it is more difficult to control. The choice belongs to the player, of course; but it is said that training with the larger one improves the player's ability to control the ball.

There are two compressions of ball, a high and a medium. Only players of great strength should use the high, for that sweet feel of club striking ball is spoiled when the ball is too hard for the striker.

PART TWO — TECHNIQUE: BASIC

CHAPTER 5 — BASIC PREPARATION

The golf swing is made at a stationary ball; which, strangely enough, makes the game more difficult than if the ball were moving. There is no opportunity for the golfer who has a mishit to blame 'an unlucky bounce', 'an unseen spin' or even having been 'wrong-footed'. Ninety per cent of a good swing is decided before the player starts the actual movements into the swing; and the same could be said for a bad swing.

From the instant a player takes the club into the hands a process begins which carries on until the end of the swing's follow-through is achieved. The process or routine becomes such a habit that good players are quickly identified by their habitual movements. Indeed, many a humorous impersonation has been based on a great player by golf instructors conducting a teaching clinic.

The following pages will instruct you in how to prepare properly a foundation of knowledge from which your golf swing may blossom. Without this knowledge, or without its parts being acquired in the correct order, there is little hope for anyone to develop a consistent method of swinging the club. And since so high a percentage of good swing is determined before the 'off', great care should be taken to study the following information.

The theory of swing is here presented as if by a teacher to a complete novice: in fact, in the very order in which a world-class tournament player would examine his own swing, should it be misfiring. There is as little point in learning and building a golf swing in the wrong order, as there is in an expert's seeking a fault in the complex movements of the actual swing when the fault could well lie in the pre-swing setting up!

CHAPTER 6 — THE CLUBFACE

The striking surface of a golf club is known as the clubface. The golfer must be able to recognise when his clubface is straight — because a fraction 'out' may mean many yards of inaccuracy when the ball arrives at the end of its flight.

Setting straight a wooden club is not difficult, for its design has made it virtually correct. Simply placing its sole evenly on the level ground should make the face true for aiming at the target. The damage comes as the player takes up the grip and removes the eyes from the clubface; continual glances back to it are then required.

The 'iron' clubhead is often called 'the blade' and, just as it is a simple job to be straight with a wood, so it is easy to be crooked with the iron. The line of the blade's leading edge must be exactly at right angles to the line of the target. Once more, continual regard must be given as the grip is taken up that the leading edge stays true.

Whether the chosen club be 'wood' or 'iron', its angle of loft must be allowed to show. If the shaft of the club is leaned forward, the elevating qualities of the clubface to the ball are reduced; and if the shaft leans back, they are increased.

Great care must be taken to see that the head sits true on the surface of the green and that the shaft leans neither forward nor back. The ball does best when it rolls from a true, flat surface.

The leading edge of the club, be it a wood or an iron, should be set at right angles to the ball-to-target line, as in Fig. A.

*Fig. B. is how it appears when described as **closed** to the ball-to-target line.*

*Fig. C. is when it lies **open** from the line.*

Beginners should make constant visual reference to the leading edge when getting set-up to play a shot. It is very easy, when fiddling about with the complexities of the golf grip, to find the leading edge has turned away from square. The danger, then, is that he will turn his wrists as a means of straightening the club, which will mis-direct the shot.

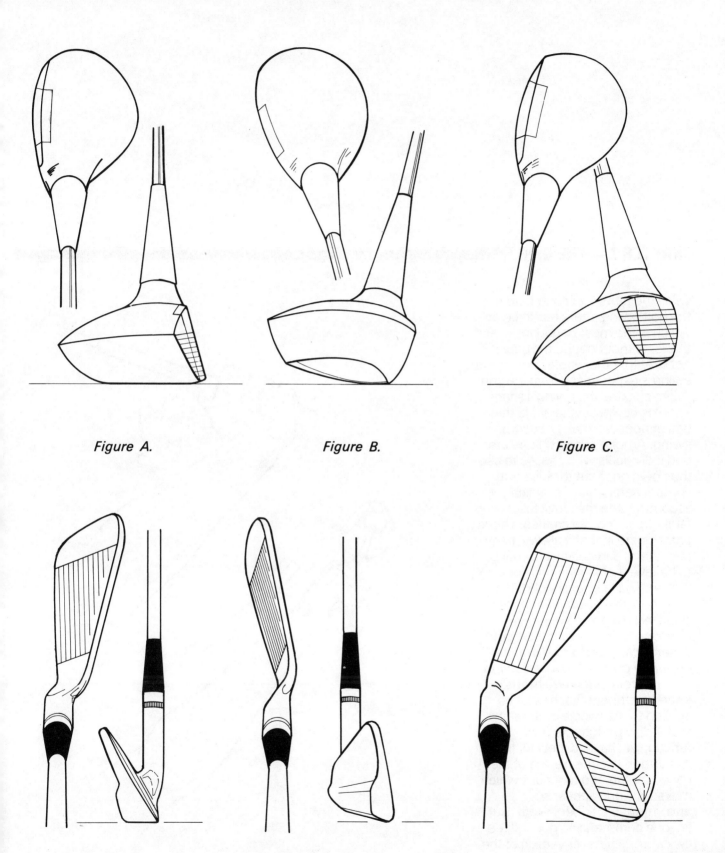

Figure A.

Figure B.

Figure C.

CHAPTER 7 — THE GRIP

Of all the parts that contribute to the golf swing, there has to be one which is *the* most important — and this is, without doubt, the grip. It is not only that the whole 'feel' of the swing is experienced from the grip; it also dictates the swing's shape. There is no way in the world that a bad gripper can make a superb swing. Among experts, there are odd individuals who choose to use their own grip; but they live with compensatory factors, which accommodate the inevitable swing faults their grip has created. This is unfortunate in that it allows many beginners, particularly the young, to believe that a good grip does not matter. The learner should believe that *though a good grip cannot guarantee a good swing, it contributes more to it than any other factor, and a bad grip will certainly guarantee a bad swing!*

The role of the two hands is entirely different. Each must be applied to the handle of the club so that it may perform its own function yet have respect for that of its partner. It is the placing of the hands for the two functions which makes the grip appear so uncomfortable to begin with. But anyone commencing golf will feel awkward, whatever version of the grip is arrived at; so why not use

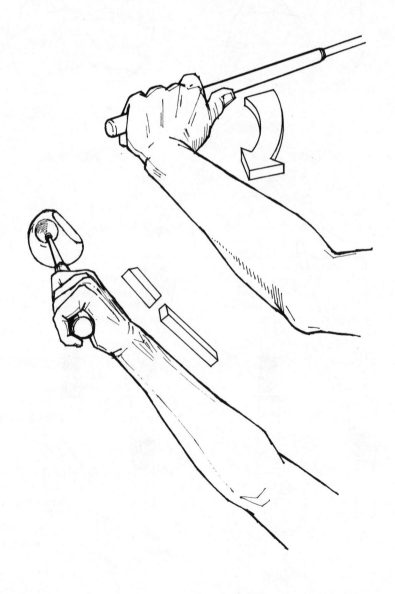

the correct one from the start? Regular golfers who suffer from irregular results should pay particular heed to the information in this chapter, for their problem is more likely to be here than anywhere else; and subsequent chapters which show the function of the swing will also show the need for good grip.

The Role of the Hands
All the movements of the body should be motivated by the arms swinging the club in an arc around it; and the hands use the club weight to effect this.

At the same time the hands must develop, by breaking the line of the arms and shaft, a source of power that will act over and above the power generated in the arc and so create even more club speed. They must also co-ordinate the timing of their preparation with the timing of the body movements they are motivating!

The Left Hand
The left hand takes its place on the handle of the club first. Bear in mind that it is there to give a guiding authority to the pair, and that its arm has a much simpler role

to perform.

The club passes from the base of the palm, pressed into the callus pad, at an angle down through the fingers, to approximate a continuation of the forearm line.

The callus pad being the centre of three sections allows the strong butt of the hand to 'sit' down on the handle from above and the end three fingers to curl up from beneath: a movement that gives total authority to the hand and engages the muscles up the underside of the forearm.

The angle of the handle passing from callus pad through

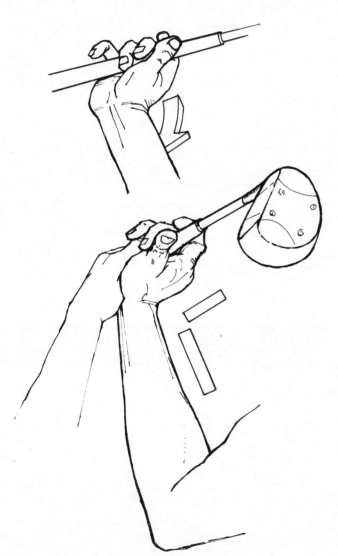

The grip taken for each hand differs because of the entirely separate roles they perform together.

The left hand is cocked at the wrist and remains in a supporting role. The right, with its more supple finger grip, is able to hinge back on its wrist in preparation to whip through!

the fingers promotes a slight separation of the index finger from the others adjoining it to the thumb, which is sealed down just over the top of the grip. In addition to being a preparation for the fitting of the right hand, this position gives a certain additional sense of 'feel', which would be lost if the handle ran entirely through the palm.

It is at this point that the player should be referring constantly to the clubface and also making sure that the correctly fitted left hand shows the knuckle joints of the forefinger and middle finger. Only then is the back of the forearm correctly parallel to the leading edge of the clubface.

The squeezing together of the thumb and forefinger produces what is known as a *vee,* which should point just to the right of the player's face.

It should be possible for the player, having extended the left arm and club to his left at shoulder high, both horizontal, and then having undone all the fingers with the exception of the forefinger, to

If the club handle lies at the correct angle across the left hand the player may extend arm and club horizontally, then slowly open most of the fingers; the clubface should remain parallel to the back of the left hand.

A poor grip by the left hand, when tested in this manner, will have the club falling to the ground especially when the player is using the wrap over of his left thumb to secure the club.

It is not sufficient to look down on a grip, and settle because the correct two knuckles are on view. The handle must also lie across the base of the palm so that the butt end of the hand can bring pressure to apply from above.

observe that the clubface remains true, the handle being secured under the butt of the hand.

Having fitted the left hand correctly, the player should be aware of a strength in the end two fingers which appears almost to stifle the wrist's natural flexibility. It should be remembered that this, the weaker of the two wrists, is going to endure the great leverage of the club during the actual swing and is therefore built to withstand collapse. It should also be realised, even at this early stage, that good swinging comes from the left side of the body and that authority is required.

A. Side view

B. Front view

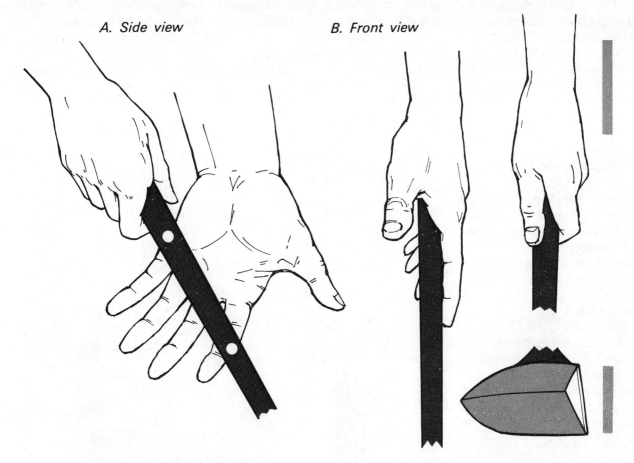

A. It is essential that the handle be placed diagonally across the left hand, fitting against the two points marked on the illustration. The point nearest the top of the handle is the seam between the callus pad and the palm: the other is against the centre section of the forefinger.

This angle allows the club to extend from the hand towards ground level with no straining of the wrist joint.

B. Care must be taken to ensure that, whilst the handle is fitting against these two points, the player continually checks that two knuckle joints are seen from above (front view). In this way, when the hand seals up the back of the left hand, the back of the left forearm and the clubface are all in line.

This is the only way a player can expect his clubface to return to 'square' at the point of impact with the ball.

The Right Hand

The right hand is the one that tends to give most trouble; for many golfers are looking for strength in this, their naturally strong hand, when in fact it must be free and flexible. The only gripping done by the right hand is delegated to the centre two fingers — that is, the end fingers of the hand, for the small finger is not counted at this stage. They permit, while being quite strong, the wrist joint to hinge freely, which would not be the case if the handle were gripped in the palm, as it is in the left hand.

It is a very simple matter to attach these two fingers, provided the player bears in mind that the palm of the right hand should be parallel to its partner. Then the spacious hollow of the palm may be placed snuggly to cover entirely the thumb of the left hand. This movement permits two very important things to happen. First, the forefinger and thumb fit on to the handle, separated slightly from the other fingers and establishing a 'pinch'; secondly, the little finger fits just behind the first knuckle of the forefinger of the other hand. Both these consequences of the

THE OVERLAP GRIP

Often too much importance is attached to the little finger of the right hand when, in actual fact, it is being 'got rid of'. It is impossible to get the thumb of the right to settle over its opposite number when the pinky is on the handle: therefore it is overlapped out of the way!

The addition of the right hand to the established left is done by the correct placing of the centre two fingers whilst the palm is angled to be parallel to that of the left hand.

It is imperative that the thumb of the left hand is safely housed under the 'trough' which forms between the thumb and palm of the right and this only happens when that little finger is lost.

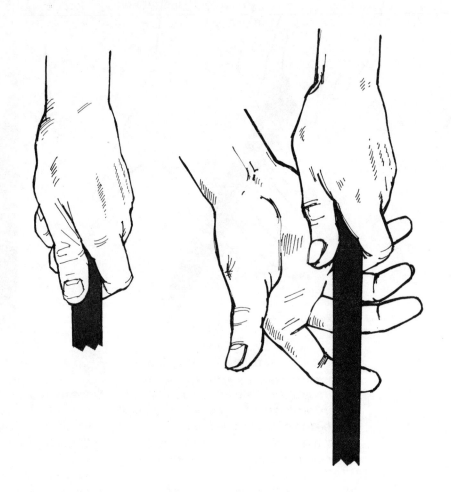

movement are essential to the correct positioning of the right hand.

Again, there is a squeezing-together of thumb and forefinger to form the vee and this also points just to the right of the player's face.

If the player removed the left hand from the grip there would exist in the right an awareness of control, feel, and agility without impression of strength which is present with the left.

The completed unit is called the **overlap grip** because of the performance of the little finger.

The grip should be firm (though never tight); and while each hand has a separate role, the grip is 'together' — the player should never feel one working from the other.

The final sealing of the right hand is a combination of the forefinger (slightly separated from the centre pair) and the thumb closing around the handle, together with the little finger hooking around the forefinger of the left.

One of the best means of checking this seal is to bring the club up in front of one's face and see that the tip of the thumb is level with the first joint of the forefinger and that they are equal, one on either side of the handle.

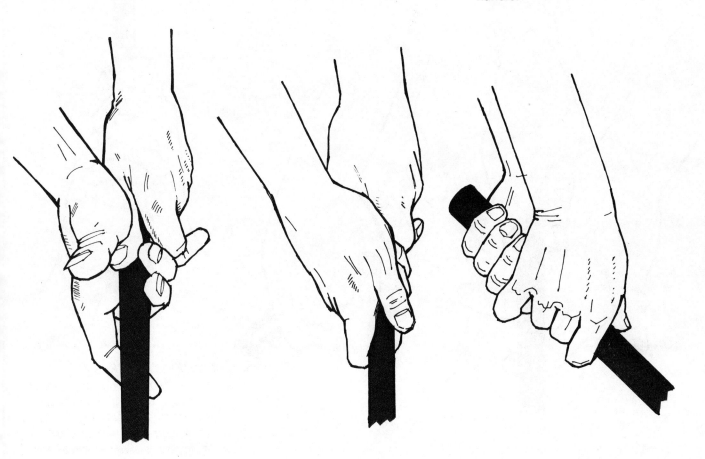

The Interlock Grip

There is one other method available where two fingers intertwine, and this is called the *interlock.* This once — popular version is currently making a bit of a comeback; which is unfortunate, since, while good players may produce a good version of it, the inexperienced are likely to undermine the quality of the left hand grip when attempting it. It tends to produce a version called *long thumb*, with the thumb of the left prodding down the grip and the 'two knuckles' of the left hand slipping back to be 'one'.

The grip known as *two-handed*, in which there is no joining, should be avoided. Even people with small hands require to lose the right hand's little finger so that the hand can get well up over the thumb of the left and prevent separation. Very small hands require thinner grips, not separation!

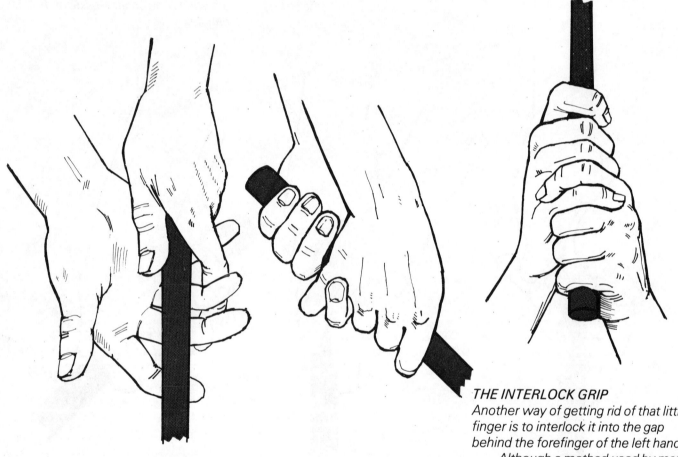

THE INTERLOCK GRIP
Another way of getting rid of that little finger is to interlock it into the gap behind the forefinger of the left hand.

Although a method used by many great players, it is vulnerable to error for it means detaching the established left hand from the handle; a move which could lead to incorrect replacement.

It is strange how this method of gripping was favoured up until the 1940s; was then overtaken (being called old-fashioned) by the overlap; and is now being used by many successful young players, both professional and amateur.

The Putting Grip

Because of the need to get the putter's near-vertical shaft into position, the handle is allowed a line through the palm of the left hand well above the callus pad, almost being secured by the thumb joint. Only the knuckle joint of the forefinger should be seen, with the thumb directly down in the centre of the handle.

The right hand is allowed to slip partly into the fingers with its thumb also on top of the grip.

If an overlap or interlock is comfortable then it should be used. Players can also reverse the overlap process, with the forefinger of the left overlapping the small finger of the right.

The best guide for a putting grip is having both thumbs on top of the handle — a position which many beginners unfortunately adopt for their other strokes with little success.

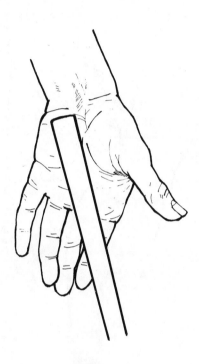 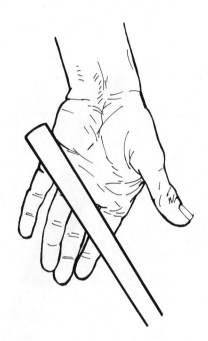 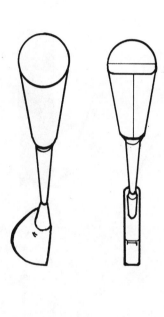

Because of the upright lie and the short shaft of the putter the handle is permitted to travel through the centre of the palm of the left hand . . .

. . . as opposed to lying across the callus pad, as in conventional strokes.

Many putter handles are designed with a flattened top surface, which encourages the player to get both thumbs pointing directly downwards.

Another advantage of having the grip through the centre of the palm is that it stops the player from squeezing the handle. A grip which is only firm enough to allow the feel of the clubhead, even in the smallest of strokes, is all that is required.

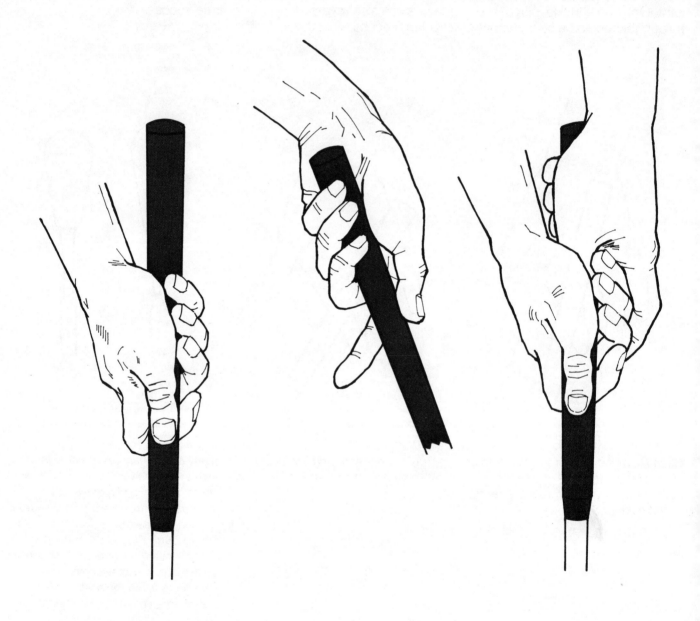

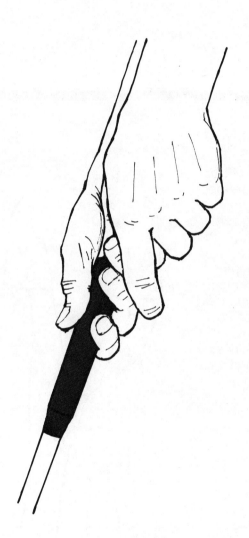

THE PUTTING GRIP
All of the fingers of the right hand are on the putter handle. Here the reverse overlap, where the forefinger of the left passes over one or two fingers of the right, is recommended. This has a strong stabilising effect on the left wrist.

Much experimenting with overlap, reverse overlap, interlock plus any other combinations should be done. Putting really is the area which brings about the golfing expression 'it is how many, not how, that counts'.

CHAPTER 8 — BALL POSITION

The importance of having the ball correctly positioned, taking up the correct stance and setting up the body must be clearly understood; for if any one of these factors is left out, or incorrectly matched, all must suffer. The stroke to be played must determine all three, with the length and nature of the club the deciding factor.

Much has been written of different choices of *ball position,* for, until fairly recently, a very different method was in existence. The golf swing then was a much wristier movement than it is today, and required the player's hands to be virtually under the chin prior to swinging. Then, the centre of the arc was a point opposite the centre of the feet, so that a shot which required any sort of a punch was played behind the centre, with only the wooden club shots going forward of centre. Today the ball is never, in a standard stroke, played from behind the centre of the stance, and even the centre itself is used only with the very shortest of iron strokes. *All other clubs are used with the ball varying between centre of feet and left heel.* The following pages will explain why this must be.

The fact of the whole matter is this: an isosceles triangle with its base across the player's shoulders (which tilt according to length of club and width of stance) would, at its vertex point, show the extreme point of the swining arc.

Each golf club according to its length and lie commits the player to adjust the width of the stance together with the angle of slope across the shoulders. The shortest club engages the narrowest stance and has the shoulders almost on level; the longest club, with its demand for strength and balance, requires the widest stance and the greates angle of slope from the shoulders.

The modern need for less activity in the left wrist during the swing, added to the right hand being applied to the handle some four inches below the left, cause the shoulders to tilt, so that even on the shortest of iron strokes the point of the isosceles is bound to be opposite a point forward of the centre of the two feet; and that is the maximum point of the swinging arc of that particular club. Many mistakes are made when golfers who still believe the ball should be played 'back' in the stance bring the hands back, too; this only serves to weaken the left wrist. *All standard strokes should be played with the left hand in line*

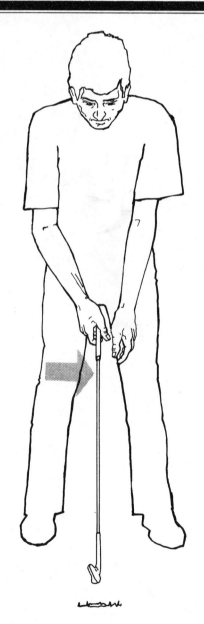

with the left thigh!

In the case of a short-iron shot, when the ball is placed opposite the centre of the stance, it is well back from the point of the triangle, so encouraging a downward blow of clubhead through the ball (as desired by players who used to play it from opposite their back foot). At the other end of the scale, with the wooden clubs, the broad stance and the added height of left shoulder above right caused by a greater reach, take the point of the triangle to a point beyond the left

foot — so disproving the old belief that a ball hit with a driver is hit consciously on the upswing. No tournament player would ever admit to feeling that his clubhead has been down to its base and is on its way up the other side when it catches the ball; he catches it on the way to the 'very forward base' of his swing. The more skilful the player the more forward his hands may travel before contact is made; which is why we hear of 'the professional's forward ball position' as against 'standard'.

Once a player has learned how to grip the club and where to position the ball for each club he should adopt the technique of introducing the club towards his left hand, whilst it remains at a point opposite the left thigh. This means that the shaft of the club will slant back towards the more centrally-positioned balls: an angle which decreases as the ball position moves forwards for the longer shots.

All of the strength of a shot is spent the moment the line of the shaft gets ahead of the players left arm and this should not happen until after the ball is on its way. So, should the player bring his left hand back to be introduced to the handle he will promote an early flick.

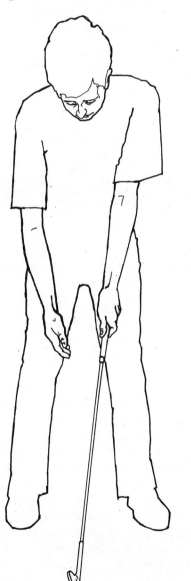

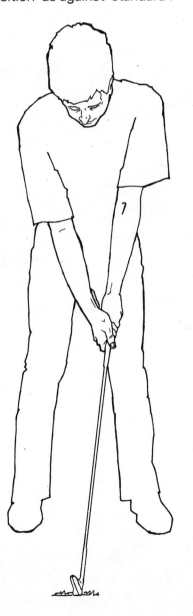

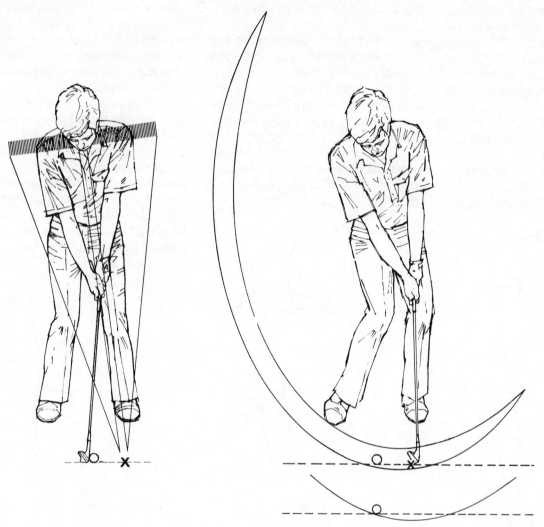

The length of the club and the width of the stance cause the player's shoulders to tilt accordingly. When this shoulder line is thought of as the base of an isosceles triangle *then the extremity of the swing arc will be at the vertex of this.*

Since, with the iron strokes requiring that the ball be struck before turf is met, the ball is positioned before the vertex point. The short irons with the smallest shoulder angle coming nearest the centre of the stance: then the ball progressing forward through the set of clubs as the left shoulder is forced higher.

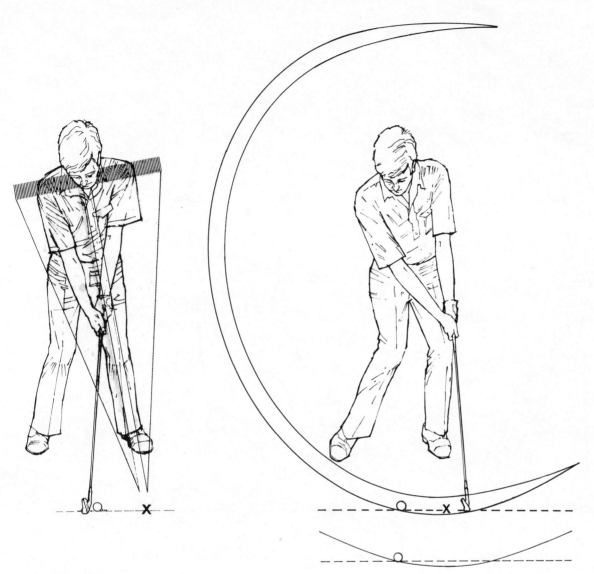

There is no mystery on how the ball is struck — then the turf is removed, in a good iron shot: the clubhead is proceeding towards the point of its fullest extension. Even the driver catches the ball slightly on the downswing, though its flatter angle of swing has this almost level with the ground; nevertheless a tee peg is necessary and the ball must be positioned well forward in the stance, and the clubface must have several degrees of loft angle!

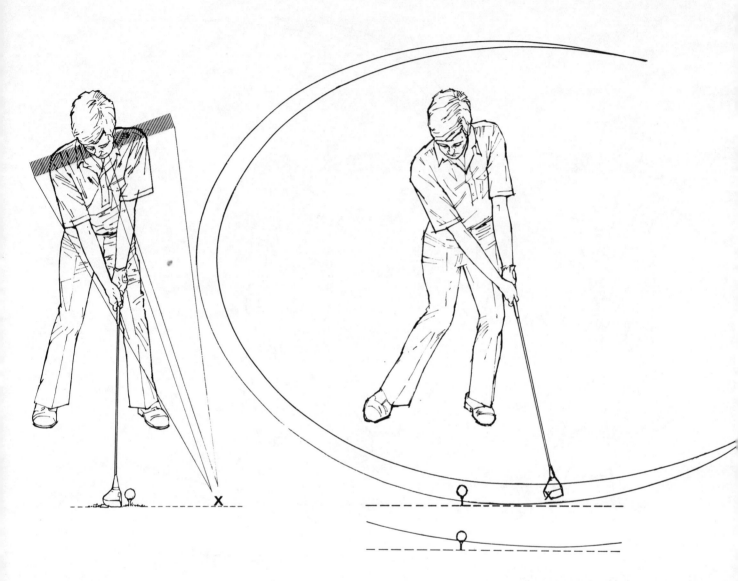

CHAPTER 9 — WIDTH OF STANCE

In order that the shoulders may gain their correct angle to direct exactly where the base of the arc will be, the stance width must be correct. A *short-iron* stroke requires a steep descent into the ball by the clubhead, which can only happen if the shoulder angle is very slight. Therefore a narrow stance is taken up, in which the width is less than that of the shoulders. This allows the hands to be in line with the inside of the player's left thigh and yet allows him the feeling that a ball opposite the centre of his feet is still behind what will be the centre point of his arc.

The *middle iron,* being longer, draws the player away from the ball and raises the left shoulder, giving a feeling of authority. To accommodate this, the stance widens to almost, (but not quite) shoulder width. The raising of the shoulders takes the base point of the arc forward, and with it the ball position. The hands will position themselves between inside and centre of left thigh, still encouraging a descending blow.

Long irons and *fairway woods* extend the width of the stance to exactly that of the shoulders. A frontal view of the player, with the left shoulder distinctly higher than the right, would show the line from shoulder to clubhead as straight; which indicates that the ball, now almost opposite the left instep, is still a fraction behind the base point of the swing, encouraging a blow which is only slightly descending.

The *long-shafted driver,* which requires the shallowest approach to the ball, takes the width of stance beyond that of the shoulders giving their maximum tilt. The additional reach, permitted by the ball's elevation by a tee peg, takes the ball's position to opposite the big toe of the left foot. Now there is practically no descent as the club sweeps on its shallow journey towards its base point.

Lining up correctly means more than just being aware of where the flag is and aiming the clubface towards it. There is much more to it than that, for an incorrectly aligned shoulder position or bad placing of the feet may make it absolutely impossible for the clubface to travel through the ball as intended.

The desired 'square-to-the-target' line up where the shoulders, arms, hips, knees and toes are all parallel to an imaginary line, drawn from the target through the ball, is more easily found if the following procedure becomes routine.

The leading edge of the club should be introduced to the ball simultaneously with the right foot taking up its intended position. Doing so allows the player continual visual reference to the target and at the same time makes him very aware of the squaring up of his shoulders.

The bringing 'into line' of the left foot and leg as the final movement avoids the danger of a closed stance occurring.

This procedure is almost the standard practice of tournament professionals, particularly those from the United States.

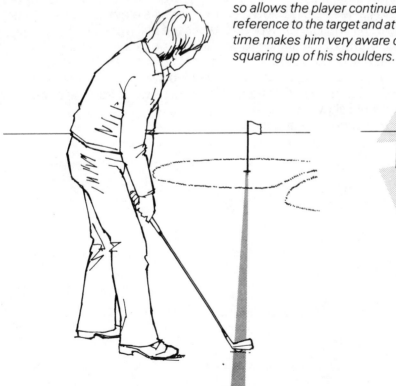

It should be appreciated that there are two halves to the body when golf is the subject: the upper body and the lower, divided (conveniently, for argument's sake) by a belt. It is perfectly correct in golf to have one of these halves deliberately off-target while the other is on. This is even required, when certain types of strokes are being played; though for the moment we will consider only the orthodox, which should be thoroughly understood and conscientiously sought.

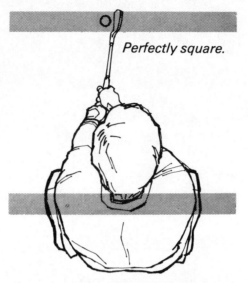

Perfectly square.

Upper Half

The upper part of the body must be guided on to a line parallel to that on which the ball would travel to the target, for out of the shoulder line comes the swinging-direction of the club. Should the shoulders point on a line off to the right, they are called 'closed'. Off to the left is 'open'; and most desirable, which is direct, is 'square'.

Lower Half

Ideally, the thighs, knees and toes should be in direct line, parallel to the ball-to-target journey. As in the upper half, off to the right is closed; to the left, open; and direct is square.

Together

In all straightforward strokes, the player should attempt to have the upper half straight but may match it with a lower half slightly open. This encourages the bottom half to lead in the crucial first movements of the downswing, when the ball is actually going to be hit.

While neither half should ever turn away closed, it is essential that the bottom half never does; for this weakens the body turn in the backswing and poses a barrier for the returning down and through movements.

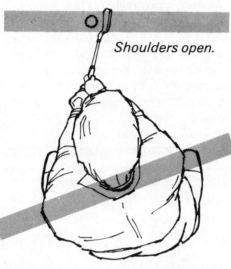

Shoulders open.

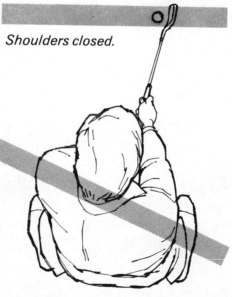

Shoulders closed.

A player, whose toes are on a line parallel to the 'ball-to-target-line', may have his shoulders accidentally turned out of line. Since the swinging arc of the club is directed by the line of the shoulders it is essential to have them square!

If the shoulders are accidentally 'open' the swingpath of the club will be led across the intended line to the target from out to in. Either a pulled shot, when the clubface is true to the swingpath, will result or, if the clubface is a little open, a slice will occur.

Should they be accidentally 'closed' then the clubhead will swing across the target line from in to out: a push, when the clubface is true to the swingpath or a hook, should it be closed, will result.

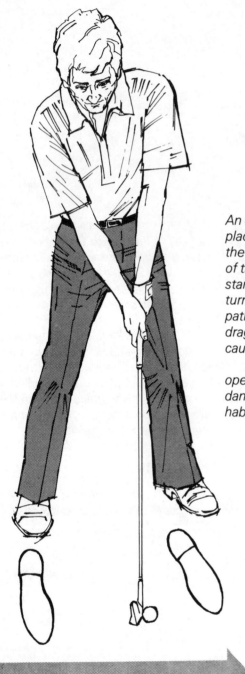

An open stance: should the feet be placed so that, were a line drawn along the toes, it would point away to the left of the target, then it is called an open stance for it has the opportunity of turning the body away from the true path of the swing. Such action tends to drag the clubface across the ball and cause it to be 'open' also!

Many professionals use a slightly open stance, favouring it to the dangerous closed stance which has a habit of creeping in.

A square stance: if a line were drawn along the toes and it lay exactly parallel to the ball-to-target line, then it is called a square stance and this is ideal as a means of simplifying the swing and the direction in which it sends the ball.

Aiming the feet is very much a habit so golfers when practising should regularly lay a club on the turf absolutely parallel to their target line, and just beyond the balls being struck. By constantly checking that their stance remains in line with that shaft a square stance will become normal.

A closed stance: when a line drawn along the toes points away to the right of the intended ball-to-target line then it is a closed stance: it tends to bar the player from getting a proper turn through to the target due to the impeding left side. Also, the clubface, which has then to turn in order to send the ball straight, is often forced to close, too!

The closed stance is one of the most destructive faults in golf and should be avoided.

CHAPTER 11 — POSTURE

The swinging of a golf club requires a great deal of movement from almost all the body's muscles. In order to perform their function with rhythm and do it consistently, balance is required. This comes from the poise of the player, established in the setting-up and maintained through the motion. Only from an athletic posture can these requirements be fulfilled.

Correct posture is done in two stages, once again separating the two halves of the body, for it is necessary to get the upper half into its correct angle before the lower half gains its flexing position.

The angle of the spine leaning

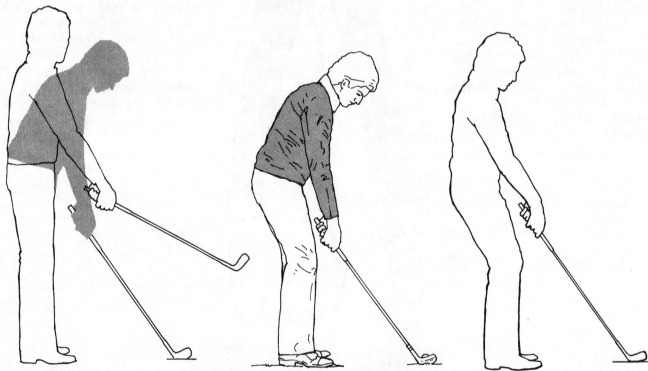

There must be two distinct movements to achieve good posture. First, the body must tilt forward from the waist, the amount determined by the length of the club. Only then do the legs flex, as the second stage.

Then the shoulders are above a point on the ground which is forward of the toes. This is necessary to permit an athletic movement as well as providing a position for the hands and wrists where they may 'feel' the swing.

Should the suggested process be reversed, with the legs flexing first, the spinal angle will be too upright and the shoulders will not be sufficiently forward. A sluggish swing is bound to result.

over, which is determined by the length of the club being used, will govern the angle at which the club travels up and down. It is of the greatest importance that this be established first. The player must therefore bend over from the belt until the clubhead is on the turf

behind the ball. The head should feel a bit 'chin up' and the wrists a bit down, which puts a feeling of sharpness into the posture.

The second stage is the gentle flexing *not bending* of the legs, which will balance the body weight, just behind the balls of the

feet. This movement will soften the spine and take the pushing down of the hands away. The left hand will be approximately four inches from the left thigh, gradually getting closer until the irons are about two inches away.

The player may turn the head

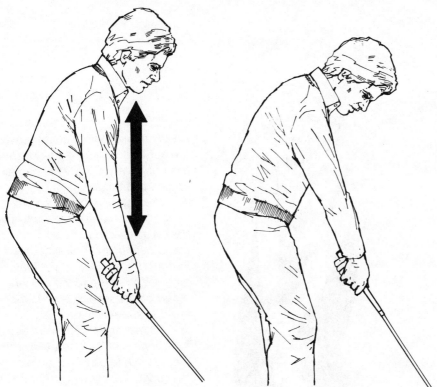

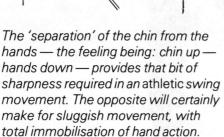

The 'separation' of the chin from the hands — the feeling being: chin up — hands down — provides that bit of sharpness required in an athletic *swing movement. The opposite will certainly make for sluggish movement, with total immobilisation of hand action.*

This separation makes the player very aware of a straightness in his left arm and this is a definate aid to good swinging.

Allowing the wrists to 'float' upwards at the address actually destroys the left arm, and the elbow has no choice but to buckle during the backswing.

The slight tilting of the head, so that the left eye is closer to the ball than the right, encourages a squarer line-up of the shoulders and helps the player gain a full shoulder turn in the backswing.

Although many great golfers use this head tilt — Jack Nicklaus being the best known — it should never be exaggerated, for it may cause the player to drop his left shoulder too much as he makes his backswing; then the club could climb much too steeply out of plane.

One thing that should never be done is to tilt the head in the other direction, so that the right eye is closer than the left. This tends to cause a lateral movement, rather than a turn, of the shoulders.

slightly, giving the impression that the ball is being looked at from the left corners of the eyes, for this encourages two things; it stops the shoulders from turning away *open*, and also encourages a good turn of the body in the backswing.

One of the best pieces of advice towards gaining good

posture for experienced golfers is to place the body, arms and clubs *in the position desired at impact* — just as if it were a still photograph being posed for. Body, arms and clubs are then very close to the exact position that should be taken up before starting the swing. After all, why start off differently, if the

pose is what is to be achieved?

The *posture* is the final stage of what is called the *set-up* — the point at which the player is ready in body and mind to make a swing and send the ball off towards its destination.

Ideally the complete posture prior to the actual swing taking place should resemble very closely the desired impact positions.

It is astonishing how many golfers, when demonstrating how they would wish to be positioned at the impact point, look like Arnold Palmer or Gary Player: yet they proceed to set up to the ball with no resemblance whatsoever to the attitude shown.

Palmer and Player were two of the forerunners of 'setting-up' as they would wish to carry on: a welcome trend which is showing more and more in good players for it is sensible to condition the start for what is about to happen.

A perfect 'top of the backswing' position. Sam Torrance of Scotland at the point where 'all is ready'. Now the attack begins.

(SportApics Ltd.)

Each of the stages of *setting up* will be wasted if the player attempts to swing the club in an arc that is 'out of plane'.

Arc describes the size and shape of the part circle the clubhead makes during the swing.

Plane is the angle on which the arc moves up and down then up again as it *backswings, downswings* and finally *throughswings.*

Fortunately, nature makes it easy for the golfer — the plane is virtually self-finding. It is decided by the tilt of the spine, which in turn is decided by the length of the club and the height of the golfer.

The short shaft of the short iron, with the near-level shoulders, brings the spine over. The backswing will make quite a steep ascent, descent, then ascent again as it goes through.

At the other extreme the long shaft of the driver, bringing up the left shoulder and extending the hands away from the body, will straighten the spine considerably. Therefore the shoulder turn will automatically be flattened, as will the entire arc from start to finish of the swing.

The correct spinal angle, determined by the club being used, remains constant from the set-up — through the backswing preparation — at impact — and is still there at the completion of the follow-through.

The awareness of this constant angle should be developed so that it is effected with every practice swing as well as every shot. During practice sessions hold the follow-through position until the ball lands, then check that the spine is on the correct slant.

An Elementary Understanding

Make a good set-up to a ball with any club, then drop it from the grip and point the forefinger of left hand at the ball. Swing the other arm up to point its forefinger in exactly the opposite direction. That is a very good way of gaining a beginner's feel of *plane*. Then, by swivelling the body to reverse the positions, you will easily grasp how *plane* exists on both sides of the swing.

A More Accurate Understanding

As with most elementary information, a tolerance must be allowed for inaccuracy. There is, of course, a more accurate description of *plane*. The elementary analysis would prove accurate were the shoulders on a level at the start and if both hands performed the same function. But in fact the left shoulder's added height at set-up *plus* the hinging back of the right hand during the backswing, provide a line of plane which on the top of the backswing preparation would not be found pointing at the ball from directly across the top of the shoulders, as the 'elementary' version would suggest. It would be found pointing from the top of the *right* shoulder, through the underside of the left, to the ball. This is because, at that point of the arc, the left side of the body is preparing to pull through, with the under muscles in their strongest position.

So much for the development of good golfing muscles may be done without a club. For example, an excellent means of getting the basic understanding of 'swing-plane' is to turn and tilt the body so that the left forefinger points at the ball, with the other forefinger pointing in exactly the opposite direction. Then swing the arms and shoulders back and forth on that tilted circle. Exercise in this manner will educate the muscles to maintain the spine on its angle.

It should be understood from the outset that it is the angle of the spine, altered by the varying length of the clubs, which determines the uprightness of the swing plane. Any player who, with his spine at the wrong angle, swings off in the hope of determining the plane by an independant lift of the arms, will find that the separation of direction will lead to inconsistency.

The spine leaning forward towards the shorter shaft of the iron creates the angle which determines the plane on which the club circles the body.

At the top of the backswing a line, drawn from ball to club shaft, should pass through the underside of the left shoulder and the topside of the right . . .

. . . the less tilted spinal angle, when the longer wood is in use, allows the flatter plane to take place. Nevertheless the line would pass through the same points.

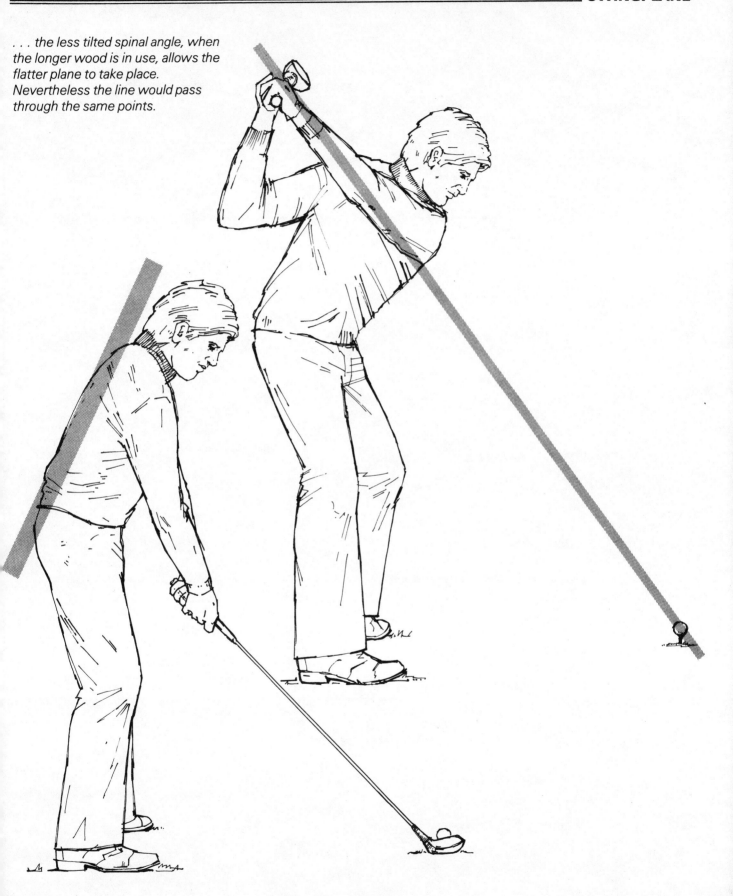

PART THREE — TECHNIQUE: SWING-BUILDING

The best way in which this manual can help both the beginner, who is building a swing, and the experienced player, who may be seeking either improvement or just a cure, is to show clearly how one swing may be built and how only the varying lengths of the clubs, together with the altering ball positions and widths of stance, make the necessary differences.

Golf is actually played in two distinct parts. In the first part, by means of the player's action and the design of the club, a ball is deliberately spun into the air and sent distances accordingly. In the second, the ball is simply pushed forward in search of roll: when done on the green, this is called *putting*; or from the fringe of the green *chipping*.

It is sensible for a novice to learn golf in reverse. That is to say, putting and chipping should be mastered before you attempt to break into the art of playing shots. Once a sense of rolling the ball is established, the movements which cause the ball to arc — from small strokes called *pitching* (the first backspinning shot in golf) up to full shots — are more easily introduced.

Aspects of technique are therefore covered here in the following order:
PUTTING
CHIPPING
PITCHING: up to SHORT IRONS
           up to MIDDLE IRONS
           up to LONG IRONS
           up to FAIRWAY
           WOODS
           up to DRIVING

Getting that swing shaped properly when the muscles are young is good advice. 12-year-old Stuart Betteridge, a pupil of the author, shows the four quite classic positions of the swing which would be a credit to any golfer. 1. The perfect set-up: head high, with the left eye just that bit closer to the ball; arms extended, but not stretched; shoulders, forearms, knees, and toes all in line.

(Betty Black)

2. The top of the backswing: head still high; left arm and wrist perfectly in line; club just short of horizontal to show control; left heel off the ground — yet the right leg remains flexed.

3. Through past the chin: note the clubhead extending on after the ball; the right heel off the grass permitting the hip and leg to get clear through.

4. A perfect end to a perfect swing!
(Betty Black)

CHAPTER 13 — PUTTING AND CHIPPING

Though it would be true to say that a person with a fine sense of rhythmic movement would make a better 'putter' and 'chipper', these two strokes can nevertheless be played effectively by a person lacking that natural asset. This is one of the wonderful things about the game. After all, nearly half the score is made up on and around the fringes of the putting greens; so a physically limited person who develops a skill in this part of the game can prove to be quite a competitor.

THE PUTT

Of the whole set of clubs, the putter is the only one with a true striking surface. All other clubs enjoy an angle of loft which, according to its degree, sends the ball forward with a backspin on it; the more lofted the club the more the forward thrust is, in a sense, undermined. So, whatever is applied to the ball by the vertical blade of the putter shows up in the forward movement of the ball.

Because of this unique design, the player may set his hands in the desired position on the handle and move both as one, back and forth, and thus create a putting stroke. Only the length and speed of the movement decides the distance

the ball will cover. There is absolutely no need for the footwork and body movement required in the other part of golf.

It must be the ambition of the golfer to develop a stroke that is consistent in its travelling line, both back from the ball, and through it towards the hole. That is the first essential of putting: *hitting the ball on line.*

Once a reliable stroke is established on a level surface, the player may take on the challenge of the slope on the green. A calculation must be made as to the effect a slope might have on the rolling ball and the amount arrived at is allowed for by making the normal stroke on the 'borrowed' (higher) side. Hence the expression 'looking for a borrow'. Many professionals are criticized for spending too much time in such searches; but one miscalculation can prove very expensive.

The amount allowed for borrow would be increased on a downhill putt, due to the gentleness of the roll; while the opposite would apply on an uphill putt, where the added power of the blow would cause the ball to maintain a more direct roll.

Having mastered a stroke that would roll the ball straight and true,

there is only one other factor to perfect in order to put all the putts in or around the hole; and that is the *pace* at which it leaves the putter. This requires a great deal of practice. It is the *pace* factor that causes much of the three-putting (the curse of golf), for most golfers acquire a fairly good sense of direction and would seldom be more than a couple of feet wide of the hole. It is leaving the putt yards short, or overhitting it by a similar amount, which causes the greatest problem.

Preparing to Putt

The procedure is the same as in all other golf strokes.

CLUBFACE

First, the blade is aimed either directly at the hole or wide of it in accordance with the allocated borrow.

GRIP

The 'putting grip' is taken up on the handle to allow the near-perpendicular shaft its correct angle.

BALL POSITION AND STANCE

The ball should be positioned just inside the left foot in a fairly narrow stance.

LINE-UP

Although experienced players adapt favoured stances and methods of aim, novices are best advised to have 'all things square on': shoulders, hips, knees and toes all on a line parallel to the intended travel-line of the stroke.

THE POSTURE

The posture is not necessarily the athletic one used in shot-making, and the player may reverse the normal process by sitting down on flexed legs before tilting the spine. (There is, after all, no body contribution.) It is desirable, however, to get the eyes almost directly over the ball.

By crouching behind the ball it is possible to 'read' the slope of the green, if there is one, so that allowance may be made. The amount which the player borrows on the topside of the hole varies, for several factors must be considered.

An uphill slope, which might require the 'aiming-off' of one inch when a firm stroke is required, might require three or four times that amount when going downhill, with the ball being helped by gravity.

The amount of 'borrow' necessary on a dry, slippery surface would be halved if the green were wet.

When a ball slips past the hole on the high side, in other words when it has been 'over borrowed', it is often described as having been 'missed on the professional's side'. This is because the top professionals know that a ball above the hole might just topple that little bit more, which would take it into the hole; whereas a ball which is on the low side can never turn up hill.

Another point to be learned from the professional is that he doesn't hit the ball hard at the hole, preferring to stroke the ball towards it. A hard rap has only one way in, when it strikes the back of the cup. The gently rolled ball may topple in from the sides also.

Though there are many individual techniques used in putting, which have led golfers to believe that this department cannot be taught, there is one factor which appears to be fairly common among the best professionals. The left forearm and the back of the hand do not break as the player strokes the putter towards the hole. This method combats the nervous 'twitch' often experienced with short putts when the player is under pressure.

A simple practice device is to tape a drinking straw to the back of the wrist and hand, and to stroke balls without folding it.

This, of course, should only be practised with putts of up to five or six yards. Any putts of a longer distance will require some freedom in the wrist to help the ball roll the greater distance. Nevertheless, the wrists are better slightly firm rather than sloppy.

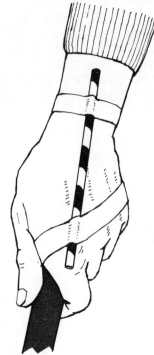

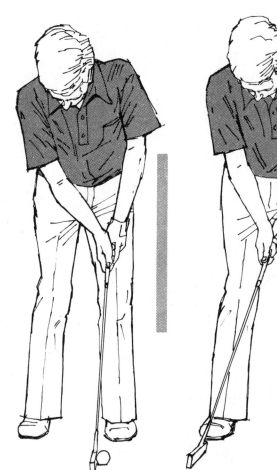

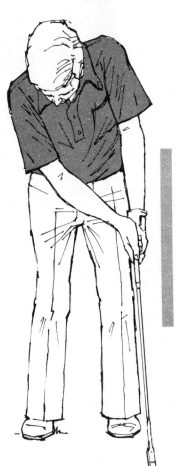

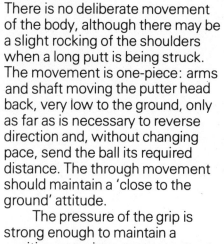

THE STROKE
There is no deliberate movement of the body, although there may be a slight rocking of the shoulders when a long putt is being struck. The movement is one-piece: arms and shaft moving the putter head back, very low to the ground, only as far as is necessary to reverse direction and, without changing pace, send the ball its required distance. The through movement should maintain a 'close to the ground' attitude.

The pressure of the grip is strong enough to maintain a positive one-piece movement yet gentle enough for the player to 'feel' the weight of the putter's head.

THE CHIP
The 'chip' is used *only* when a putt is out of the question. Merely being off the green is not the ruling factor here. If the grass is fairly short and a putt is possible it should be done, for it is the safest of all shots — and often a poorish putt-up proves to be as close as a fairly good chip.

The 'chip' is a stroke that pushes the ball forward in the same way as a putt; but in which the ball is given some elevation by the clubface loft. The backspin (applied only by the blade's loft) carries the ball over the fringe grass, which cannot safely be covered with a putter, and when the ball makes contact with the green the spin is converted into a roll.

The beauty of this stroke is often not fully realised. Many golfers associate it with one club, a 5 or 6, or a special 'chipping club' which has a similar loft. However, the advantage of safety in the

The caddy demonstrates the correct way to attend the flag. If the putt has been struck equally well, then it should go in.

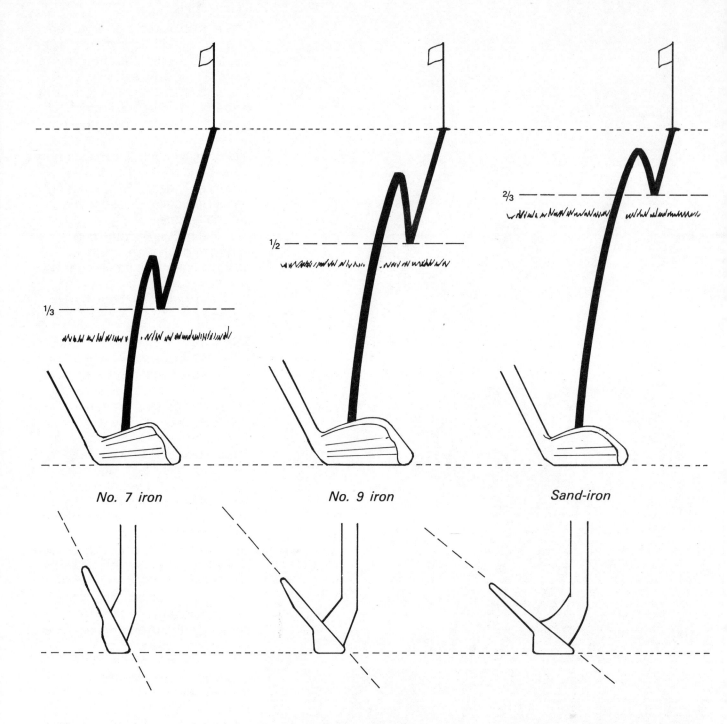

No. 7 iron   No. 9 iron   Sand-iron

Provided the left wrist does not 'break' at impact but maintains a firm one piece, back-and-forth movement with the club, then the ball is driven forward rather than upwards. The player may be choosing the correct club, assessing how much of the total journey he requires to carry the ball in the air so that its first bounce will be safely on the smooth surface of the green. Remember that the longer the amount the ball can spend rolling, the easier the shot to play!

Individuals, by practising, will find their own scale of carry-to-run per club, but here is an approximate chart.

A No. 7 iron carries $\frac{1}{3}$ then runs $\frac{2}{3}$
A No. 9 iron carries $\frac{1}{2}$ then runs $\frac{1}{2}$
A Sand iron carries $\frac{2}{3}$ then runs $\frac{1}{3}$.

The circumstances should always be allowed to dictate the club. It is foolish to discard safety in the short game for risky original strokes.

technique taught in this manual may be derived using many of the iron clubs in the set.

The method drives the ball forward.

The loft of the selected blade defuses the forward drive.

So, according to the amount of 'ground to be covered' and 'green to roll on', the correct club may be chosen.

Each individual has to find his own exact ratio of 'carry' to 'run'; but here are some examples:

A 7 iron would cause the ball to lift for one-third, and run for two-thirds of its journey.

A 9 iron would cause it to fly just less than half the total, and run the rest. A sand iron used in the same manner would make it fly two-thirds of the distance, leaving it only a third to run out.

Each club could be charted by its owner — a little practice would ensure great accuracy.

Allowances should be made to the specification for playing into an uphill as against landing on a downhill slope; for playing onto a wet, soft surface as against a rock-hard one.

Playing the chip requires that the normal golf grip is taken up. However, the left wrist should then be slightly arched forward so that the shaft appears to be leaning forward (care must be taken to see that the clubface remains square to the target line: there is often the inclination to turn it open). By maintaining this forward position of the wrist until the follow through is complete, the ball will shoot forward on landing. Loss of this angle will allow the club to flick through the ball, causing a backspin which is difficult to estimate.

It is also recommended that the hands be placed down the handle so that as much as 2 to 3 inches protrudes beyond the left hand.

Not only does this add to the player's confidence by getting him closer to the ball, it also stabilises the wrists.

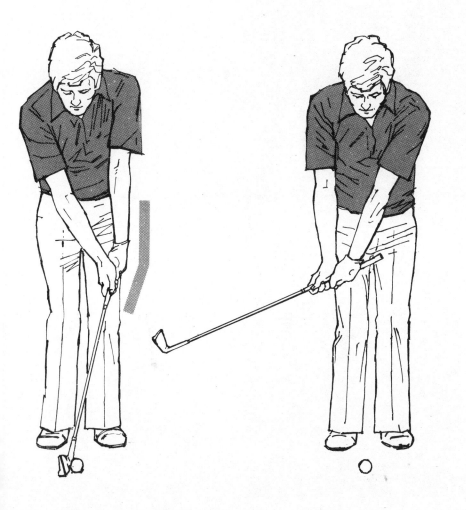

The Method

Basically, the same attitude as that adopted for putting is applied, because the club is worked back and forth along a straight *line of travel*. It is moved at one speed, with the arms and shaft staying firmly together.

Unfortunately, the angles of lie at which the various shafts leave the club heads necessitate a return to the conventional golf grip, with the attendant danger of a slight wrist movement that would cause the blade either to hit the ground before the ball or to create additional backspin (which would play havoc with the flight specifications given). Therefore, a couple of adjustments are made, to eliminate the danger.

The ball is positioned back in the narrow stance, to a point about opposite the right foot. At the same time, the left wrist joint is pointed forward and 'frozen' in that shape.

It is then merely a case of applying the rules of a putt, the firmness being determined by the journey to be covered.

The secret of success with chip and run shots is to keep the hands ahead of the shaft throughout the stroke.

CHAPTER 14 — THE SWING

It is understandable that a novice golfer might panic on seeing a bag full of clubs, believing that there must be 14 different golf swings to be learned. Indeed, the first experience many have of the game is seeing golfers on the television screen using all sorts of swings. Nevertheless, there is but one swing per person, not per club; and though there are 'variations on a theme', they are very advanced and to be learned at a much later stage.

As far as the novice is concerned, all the changing shapes of swings are the effect of a combination of three factors that affect the set-up: the length of the club in use, the ball position, and the alteration to the width of stance. What is necessary is the building of one shape of swing, and the following pages will explain how that may be accomplished.

The **first shot in golf is the minimum distance that a ball may be lofted, with every golfing muscle of the body participating.** That is the point where a chip becomes a pitch; the point where rhythm, co-ordination and skill take up.

Unfortunately, a swing cannot be built from a pitch up into a full stroke (which is how it is done) until the golfer knows what the full swing consists of. It would be like trying to imagine a percentage of something without knowing the total. Therefore, a clear understanding of that 'total' is necessary, and of the way in which the 'departments' of the swing are trained to build up in a balanced form, each contributing an equal percentage until the maximum is achieved.

It is essential to break the swing into departments, each of which plays its part in the making of the full 100% stroke. Though these departments vary in function, they work together. They set out together; they arrive together. Should they participate in the backswing preparation, they aim to make that journey in *one movement*. Should their involvements be in the throughswing, they time to complete that in yet another *one movement*. They are covered by a total shape which keeps them all as travelling companions throughout the journey, co-ordinated to exact timing and so sharing the load.

The Departments

The hands and wrists and the club.

The arms and shoulders.

The hips, legs, ankles and feet.

While there are many other muscles and areas involved in a golf swing, those given are the ones of which the golfer must be aware. They are listed in the order of greatest involvement and importance to the player.

The Duties of the Departments

THE HANDS, WRISTS AND THE CLUB

Protected by golf's orthodox grip, the hands are connected by means of the shaft to the clubface and so constitute the link between mind and clubhead. They are responsible for the latter's attitude when it contacts the ball. They decide whether there is a bit of a punch to be applied in a short iron, or a sweeping movement when a wood is in use; whether the face should be open or closed, applying the required wrist movement. They not only prepare for power in the way they cock the wrist joints, but also guide the arms and shoulders into the correct *plane* of swing, which, though dictated by the spine's angle, is not easily found. Because of their unique sense of feel, they govern the degree of involvement, not only in pace but in aggression, of all other departments. A player will reach

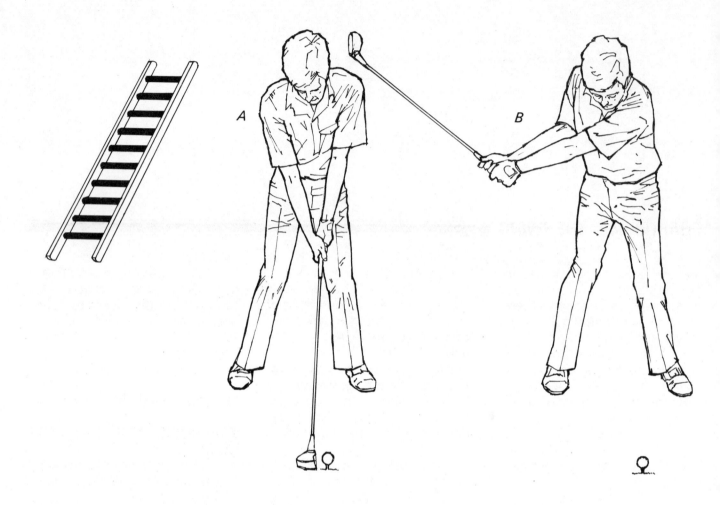

This book will show how the full swing is arrived at as the top rung of a ladder which is climbed from the smallest of percentages of movement of each of the swing's departments which grow, rung by rung, per cent by per cent, until the full percentage is achieved i.e. the full swing.

A percentage of any item can only be assessed when the maximum is known so the full swing, the top rung of the ladder, with all of its departments working to 100% must be clearly understood first. These are treated as the same for all full shots, regardless of the club for it is the length of the club and width of the stance which creates any alterations.

THE DRIVE
The combination of the longer club, upright posture; the wide stance and the forward ball position encourages the fullest of swings where all of the departments are going through their 100% potential.

A

B

THE MIDDLE IRON

The same 100% is being sought by all of the departments but the slightly shorter shaft, which pulls the posture over, together with the narrower stance and more central ball position, cause the arc to be slightly narrow and a little steeper.

C

D

E

F

G

very high standards only if blessed with 'good' hands.

ARMS AND SHOULDERS
Regardless of the stroke being played, the swing is made up of 'departments'. Some departments contribute to 'feel' and 'creativity' while others provide 'width' and therefore 'security', necessary for the consistent performance of the other departments. Many self-taught golfers over-indulge in the 'feel' and 'creativity' departments with little hope of consistent progress. Others, who may tend to overthink and over-theorise, become static by clinging entirely to 'width' and 'security', which, though providing more uniform shots, would never allow the sparkle of flair to surface.

When there is a lack of pure physical strength then a fullness of arc must be used. Chako Higuchi of Japan, past winner of the Colgate Ladies European Championship, completes this swing and shows that nothing was spared.
(Peter Dazeley)

Because of a correctly placed grip on the club the hands are permitted to prepare correctly during the back movement. From their starting position there is a gradual cocking of the left wrist, as though the thumb were being levered back towards the forearm. Meanwhile, the right wrist, because of its finger grip, is hingeing with the back of the hand going towards its forearm.

The cocking allows the left hand to contribute to power, yet encourages the movement to take place on the safe angle of the swing's plane. Were it to attempt to hinge then it would cause the clubface to turn open.

The right hand hinges back on the wrist joint ready for releasing the clubhead freely through the ball at the base of the arc. It is for this that it is being prepared.

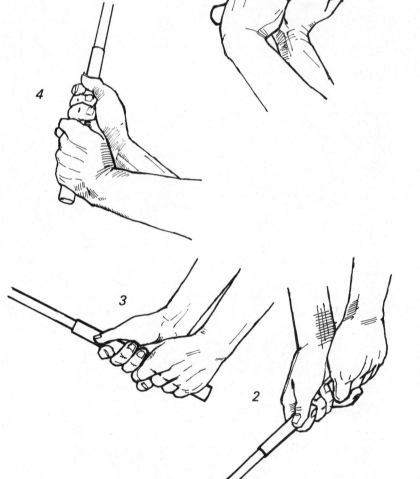

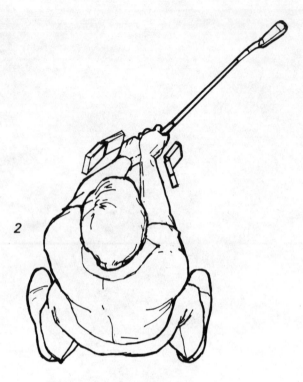

Looking down on the swinger it can be clearly seen how, as the hands and wrists set off in preparation to hit the ball they, by means of the arms, engage the shoulder turn to whatever amount is required for the type of shot being played.

Here, where a middle iron is being used, the rate and angle of wrist action is shown by hingeing blocks. In the case of a short iron where the width of the stance would be narrower, and the club handle shorter, the wrist action would show as happening sooner with a fairly limited arm and shoulder involvement and a more upright angle.

In the case of a driver the wrists would appear less active and the shoulder turn would be fuller; so the arc would be flatter.

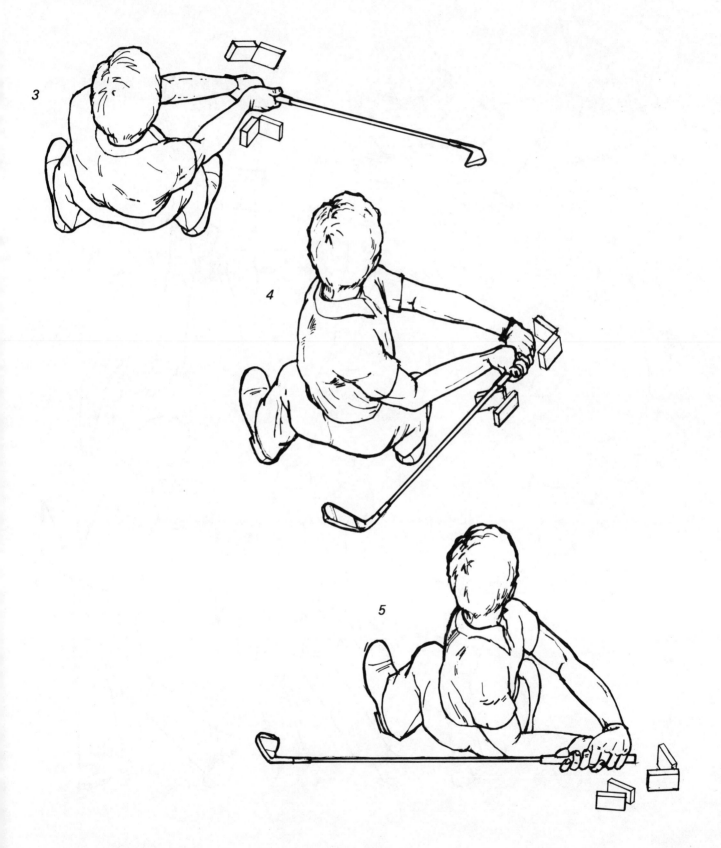

3

4

5

Arms and shoulders working together provide the 'width' and 'security' and only when not guided by the hand action would they cause the swing to be dull. Whatever the width of arc involved, it is the duty of the arms and shoulders to provide it both during the backswing preparation, and in the throughswing.

When the hands set off with the club, there is an immediate response by arms and shoulders together, the arms moving into plane and the shoulders turning to accommodate them.

While the hands dictate the speed of the movement and the power required, the arms and shoulders contribute greatly to the generation of power.

THE HIPS, LEGS AND FEET
Because of the fact that the backswing preparation is motivated from the 'belt' upwards and the throughswing from below the belt, the contribution of the hips, legs and feet appears quite minimal going back, then very lively going through.

While the hands work the arms and shoulders, the right hip, leg and foot gather the pressure by maintaining as closely as possible their 'set-up' position. This must not be misread as a suggestion that the bottom half is static, for the left instep and thigh, using the knee and ankle joints, lift and move inwards in readiness for a very smart reversal.

This lower-half preparation set off the second part of the swing, when the left hip, leg and foot drive back towards the target, aided by the right leg pushing.

Their contribution at this point allows the arc of the shoulders and arms to return safely in plane into their throughswing, and encourages the angle made between shaft and arms to remain in a powerful angle until the correct type of unwind may be safely delivered.

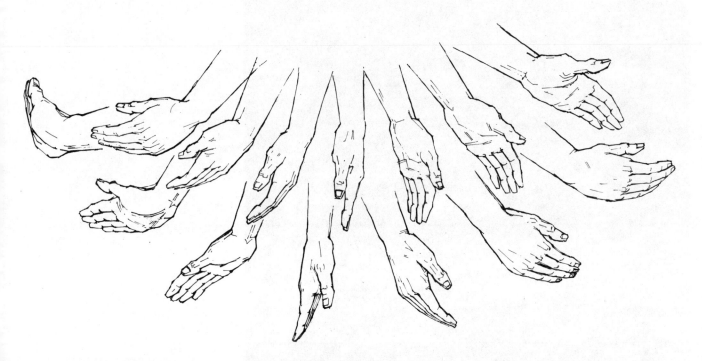

One of the best 'swing-building' exercises is done without a club where, by swinging with the palms parallel and at the same time separating the body into two halves (above the belt and below the belt), a perfect golf movement may be created.

The hands, with a constant and parallel gap between them, swing off with the arms in search of plane. Doing so brings the shoulders around into a proper turn.

The player is aware of the top half of the body making the backswing. Then by leading with the hips and legs which had quietly been drawn into position by the top half, the bottom half creates the throughswing with the top being led through.

. . . Swinging through from the exercise without using a club educates the hands to remain parallel to each other throughout the golf action.

It can be seen here how the lower hand is much more active through the bottom of the swing compared with the simple undoing of the left. Hence the reason for the different grip taken up by each hand.

Gary Player, possibly the most competitive professional who ever walked a fairway. A man who has won major championships in three decades and who looks like going on for more. There's tenacity for you!

(Essex Sports)

CHAPTER 15 — BUILDING FROM THE PITCH SHOT

Once it is accepted that a full shot is made up of 100% of each of the three *departments,* with the length of the club, the ball position and the width of the stance adjusting the potential of each, then the novice can begin to build a sound golf swing.

Close study of the following pages will also repay the experienced golfer who has difficulty in pitching short distances. What causes this problem is the fact that the club being used — ideally the pitching wedge — is capable in full swing of sending the ball a distance of, say, 100 yards (about average for a male player). Should the journey to be covered be less than this, the mind of the poorer 'pitcher' does a subtraction sum. He looks for a way of cutting down on power by weakening certain areas and, worse, applies gimmicks such as laying the blade open, turning the shoulder open, weakening the grip by showing less than two knuckles, and even leaning the weight on the right foot throughout. Each and every such move is negative and is exactly what subtraction creates.

The way to pitch well is to be *positive,* which is achieved by taking each department of the swing that creates the 100% stroke and making it co-ordinate with its companions to produce, say, 10% only.

The only complaint would come from the feet and legs, for the width of stance recommended for the short iron would not allow such small involvement. This is understandable, since width of stance contributes to power. The feet must be brought very close together and, to adjust the posture to accommodate, this move, the hands take their position down the handle.

All else remains as in a short-iron stroke; and when each department offers its 10%, a golf movement is created that will arch the ball forward approximately 10% of the player's potential: i.e., about 10 yds.

As soon as this is functioning, by the slightest of widening of the stance and moving up on the handle, 20% of all departments should be introduced. The process then continues until, in 10% and

10-yd intervals, the player arrives, as though at the top rung of a ladder, at the full 100% shot.

The benefit of this process will soon be felt by any golfer who has had trouble with this area of his game. The wedge shot he used to dread will have changed from a subtraction sum, in which the shot required represented something less than the club's potential, to (provided the journey is more than 10 yds) an addition of power. It is the increasing of power which is the only true source of the backspin we see created by the game's great players. Acceleration at impact, by a positive increase of power, sharpens the spin of the ball up the angle of the clubface.

Once the 100% of all departments is reached, the ball can travel no further than the club's maximum and it simply becomes a selection of the correct club for the journey required. Each of the other clubs is played with all departments working on their 100% basis, swing shape and size being self-adjusting at set-up by their length and lie.

BUILDING FROM THE PITCH SHOT

Using a pitching wedge, held slightly down the handle, a narrow stance is taken; then each department introduces 10% of its potential and the ball arcs and travels some 10 yards.

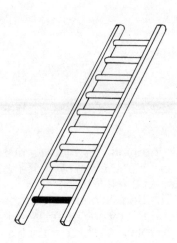

A slightly wider stance, a bit nearer the top of the handle, and 30% of all of the departments are introduced, together with an increase of pace. Then the ball arcs 30 yards.

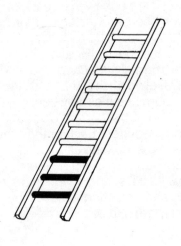

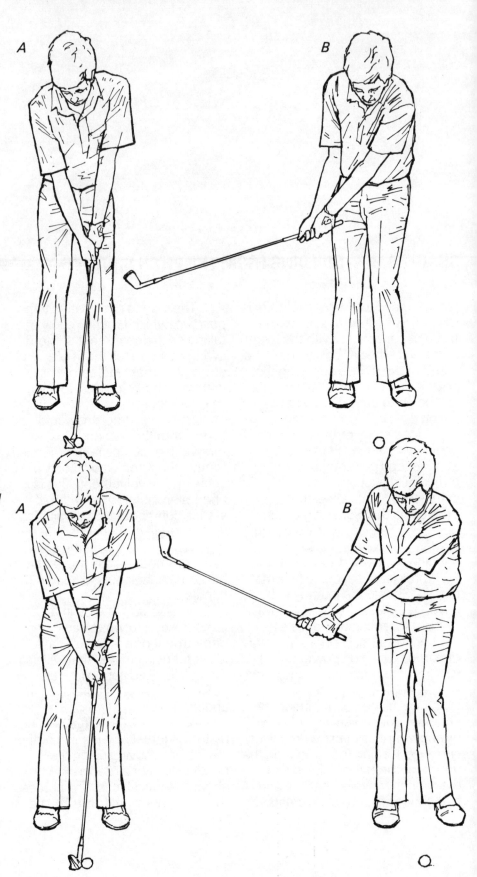

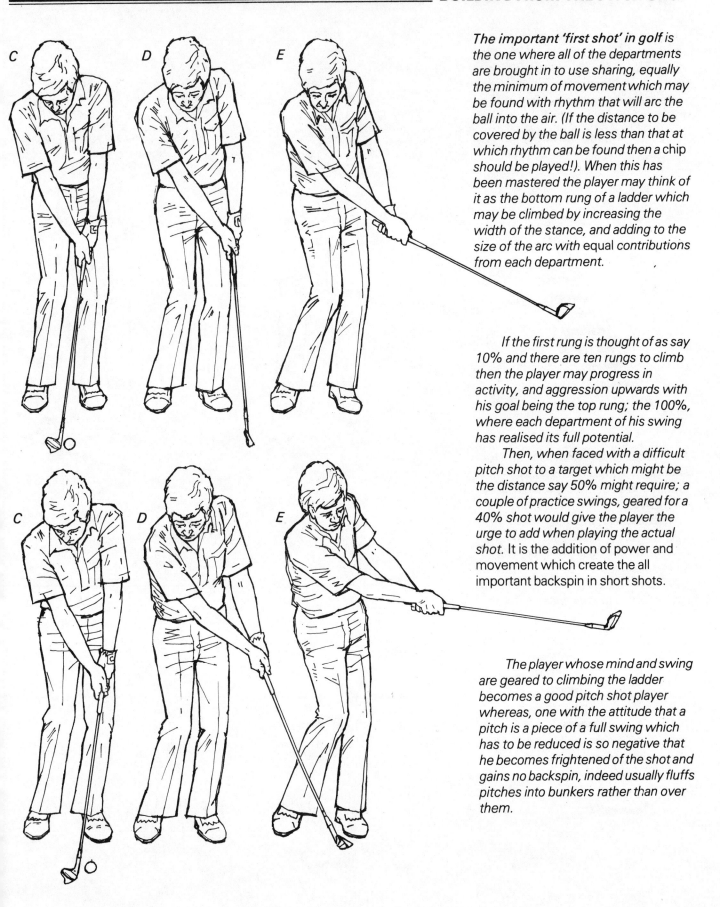

C   D   E

C   D   E

The important 'first shot' in golf is the one where all of the departments are brought in to use sharing, equally the minimum of movement which may be found with rhythm that will arc the ball into the air. (If the distance to be covered by the ball is less than that at which rhythm can be found then a chip should be played!). When this has been mastered the player may think of it as the bottom rung of a ladder which may be climbed by increasing the width of the stance, and adding to the size of the arc with equal *contributions from each department.*

   If the first rung is thought of as say 10% and there are ten rungs to climb then the player may progress in activity, and aggression upwards with his goal being the top rung; the 100%, where each department of his swing has realised its full potential.
   Then, when faced with a difficult pitch shot to a target which might be the distance say 50% might require; a couple of practice swings, geared for a 40% shot would give the player the urge to add when playing the actual shot. It is the addition of power and movement which create the all important backspin in short shots.

   The player whose mind and swing are geared to climbing the ladder becomes a good pitch shot player whereas, one with the attitude that a pitch is a piece of a full swing which has to be reduced is so negative that he becomes frightened of the shot and gains no backspin, indeed usually fluffs pitches into bunkers rather than over them.

BUILDING FROM THE PITCH SHOT

The width of stance nears its maximum for a short iron, the hands are nearly at the top of the handle and the departments all offer 70% of their potential. The pace is getting close to that of a full shot and the ball arcs some 70 yards.

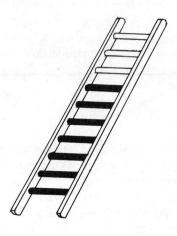

Finally the stance is the maximum for a short iron. The wedge is held at full extent and all of the departments function to the maximum such a stance and posture permit. From this 100% offering the ball arcs 100 yards and the full swing is achieved. The ladder has been climbed. From then on it is merely a case of changing of clubs and adhering to their characteristics!

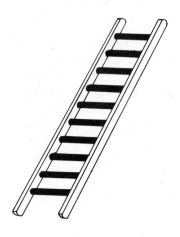

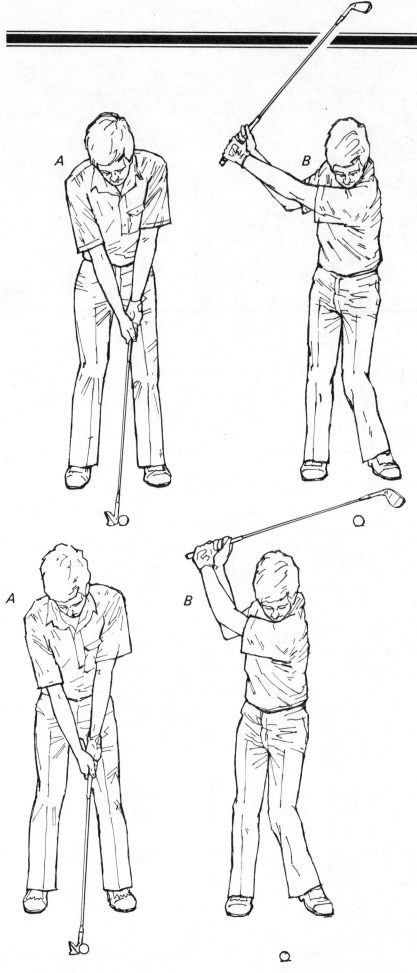

Johnny Miller, the young American whose fame arrived like a rocket in the mid-70s then disappeared like a damp squib before the decade was over. Here he shows the swing which might bring him back to the top where he belongs. There is no doubt, from the quality of this swing, that his decline is purely a mental problem. Golf, played over so many hours and over so many days demands that the player be in perfect mental conditon. This man doesn't feel that he can win — but he can!

CHAPTER 16 — THE SHORT IRONS (8, 9, PITCHING WEDGE)

Depending on the circumstances prevailing; each of the short irons may be adapted to play a part in chip and pitch shots by using the techniques already described, choice determining the trajectory and subsequent run-out on the ball. However, as part of the whole set, the short irons have their full strokes to play and the following procedures should be used.

The leading edge of the clubface is set down behind the ball, aiming square to the flag.

The ball is positoned at its most central point, opposite a square stance slightly narrower

The change which shows the swings of each club to be different is created entirely by the length of the club and the width of the stance with their effect on the posture.

The short handle of the wedge with the narrow stance, pull the shoulders forward and the arc made gives the impression of a letter U. Whereas the longer handled driver, with the wider stance and more erect posture cause a shallower, fuller turn to be made, and the arc becomes like a letter O.

There is absolutely no need for the player to force these letter shapes to happen; the club and the nature of the shot do it.

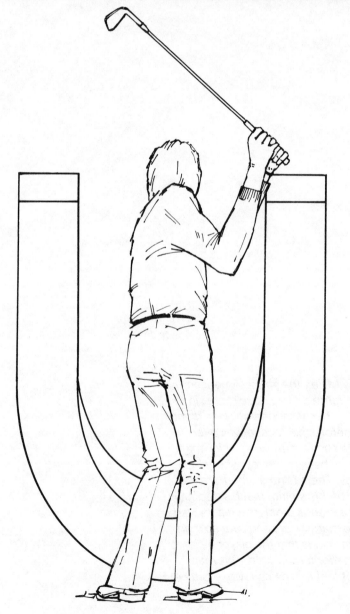

than shoulder width.

The hands are opposite the *inside* of the left thigh, causing the shaft to slant back to the ball.

The posture makes the spine lean over, which brings the hands fairly close to the left leg. This movement increases the response of the hands so they may complete their preparation to time with the shorter journey, permitted by the posture, of the arms and shoulders.

The completed set-up has dictated the length of the backswing and the steepness of the plane. While the set-up may convince the player that the hands are busier than the other departments, all departments do in fact work to their permitted full potential and provide a preparation which is about three-quarters that of a driver.

The through movement commences with a lateral movement of the hips and legs. The left heel, which might be only fractionally off the turf going back, gets down, for there can be no lateral shift with it in the air.

Because of the steepness of plane and the busier hand-work, a player may add a feeling of punch if desired; though this is not necessary and the independence of such action could lead to inaccuracy. The swing movement should be through to the finish.

The spinal angle dictates that the finish will be shorter and of a much more decisive appearance than will be the case in longer shots; and, though the player's face may turn to see where the ball is going, the head will remain *above the original point of the base* (not over the centre of the feet as is often suggested).

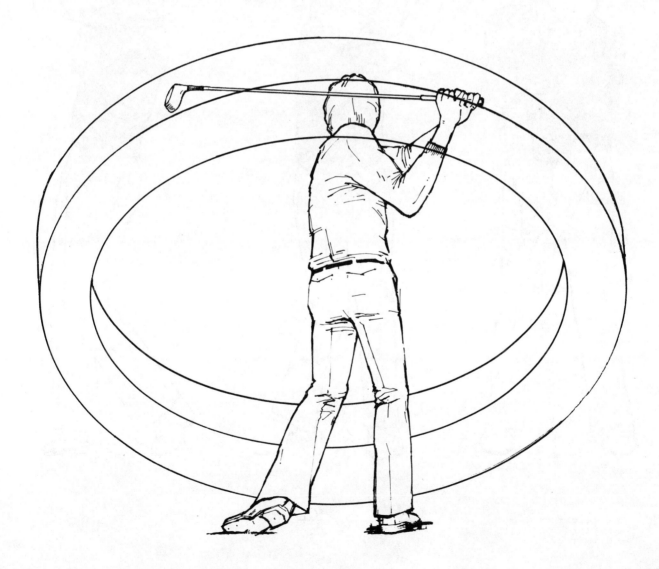

With all departments working at 100%
the full swing is achieved. Here it is
seen with a short iron: the length of
the club, the shortness of the shaft,
and the ball position make it appear
short and simple.

CHAPTER 17 — THE MIDDLE IRONS (NOS. 5, 6, 7)

Once again, the leading edge of the blade is set behind the ball, aiming square to the target. The ball position is forward of centre and the stance widens towards shoulder width.

The hands move forward to be almost in line with the centre of the left thigh. With the shafts lengthening and the spine becoming more erect, the shoulders begin to slope, left higher than right.

The effect of these measures is a dulling of the hand and wrist action and an increase in the potential of the arms and shoulders. More turn is promoted, also a slight widening of the arc, with the result that the arc's angle of plane flattens automatically with no conscious effort from the player.

The increased width of the stance provides a stronger base to support the swing enlargements. The widening is necessary not only for the backswing but for the throughswing, too. The arc filling-out will become more aggressive and the lateral transfer of the bottom half of the body requires a fairly strong, dependable footing.

The middle irons are so called because they balance between the steep downward hitting of the short-iron arc and the shallower sweep of the long irons and fairway woods. They strike through ball then turf (as the clubhead travels through the appointed ball position) in search of the point of the triangle and, having found it, continue on to the finish of the throughswing.

The finish has that look of solid authority, with the arc showing no signs of collapse, the player's eyes following the ball and his head above the base of the arc.

CHAPTER 18 — THE LONG IRONS (NOS. 2, 3, 4)

Long irons are almost woods, with their long shafts; and when the leading edge is set square behind the ball the player is encouraged, by the flatter lie of the club, to stand away.

The ball is positioned opposite a point midway between the centre of the stance and the left instep, and the stance is shoulder-width. With the hands now three or four inches away from the thigh but in line with the centre, there exists a slight angle back towards the ball.

However, with the hands away from the leg and the much more upright posture afforded by the longer shaft, deliberate hand action is completely unnecessary. At this stage the golf swing is being given over to the width-makers, the arms and shoulders, and being taken away from the more active hands and wrists.

The turning ability, although not quite as extensive as in wooden club shots (owing to their even longer shafts), is nevertheless very full indeed and the plane of the swing approaches its shallowest angle.

The power developed by such a swing requires the broader stance for, in the backswing preparation, the right leg must gather the pressures of the movement and the left leg and hip must then support the fuller throughswing and its completion.

Because the ball is positioned behind the point of the shoulder's triangle, there could still be a bit of turf taken after impact; but this is more likely to be grass than divot, with the swing continuing on in plane to a very full finish.

. . . Here, with a long iron, all the departments, still doing 100%, are appearing much fuller — only because of the longer shaft, coupled with the wider stance, and more forward ball position.

CHAPTER 19 — THE WOODEN CLUB

While the more lofted wooden clubs, 4 and 5 may be positioned back as for long irons, the driver and the 3 wood come up opposite the left heel. The difference between these last two is that the 3 wood has a stance of shoulder width, with the slant across the shoulders still dictating the base of swing to be after the ball, thus ensuring the ball is struck fractionally on the descent; whereas the driver's stance goes beyond shoulder width, which makes the ball's position on a tee peg closer to the point of the isosceles triangle.

The erectness of posture; the height of the left shoulder at set-up; the demand of width and turn on the arc: all contribute to the shallowness of the plane and all serve to reduce the hand action to its 'conscious' minimum.

At this point the golfer is more aware of the large-muscled departments and hardly conscious of the small-muscled ones which, because of their training, are nevertheless involved. It is simply that they have much more time with the biggest arc to prepare for, then contribute, their particular effort.

Many good players say how aware they are of hand-work in short irons and completely unaware with the woods; yet their hands do every bit as much work in both.

Summing Up

When the big swing, whether it be with the wedge or with the driver, has been achieved, it should be seen as 'the top rung of the ladder', or the 'last shot of golf'. The 'bottom rung of the ladder', the 'first shot in golf', was achieved when those muscles subsequently seen sending drives off from a 100% workrate first set out working gently together to the tune of 10%.

It should be understood that, for perfect balance and co-ordination of movement, the pressure of the swing — and the speed it moves — increases along with the percentages being added; the drive moving fastest of all. It is essential not to misinterpret this point. The golf swing does not build up into a frenzy: the speed of the 100% golf swing is determined by the nature of the individual. A person who is quick and fiery in temperament will swing fast certainly. But he who does most things in life as a leisurely pace will bring the same approach to his golf swing. Whatever the final pace,

therefore, it is his 100% when it reaches the full stroke; and he has built towards it from that first little pitch shot that lofts the ball with backspin: *The First Shot in Golf.*

Finally, the full flow of the departments which, due to the great length of the shaft, the widest of stances, and the very forward position of the ball, appear to be doing much more than the full short iron movement. Yet the departments continue to 'share the load' evenly.

PART FOUR — SLOPING LIES, BUNKERS AND RECOVERY SHOTS

CHAPTER 20 — SLOPING LIES

For the average golfer, sloping ground produces the most inconsistent hitting of the ball. Yet professional golfers appear to find no difficulty whether they be above or below the ball, or going uphill or downhill. The reason is quite simple. The amateur's adjustment of balance and weight distribution — an adjustment that would appear natural to counteract the

---

No it doesn't snow in Australia! Greg Norman, the leading Australian blasts his way to victory in his country's Open Championship.

(Ken Lewis)

slope — renders the body totally unable to make the correct arc to send the ball from the slope on which it lies. The professional actually argues with gravity by positioning his body line so that it is able to produce the arc required to send the ball from its situation.

There are, of course, certain severe slopes which cannot be argued with; but these are dealt with later in the chapter, under the heading of recovery strokes.

STANDING ABOVE THE BALL
This is probably the most difficult of hillside strokes, for the leaning forward of the body has such a

limiting effect on the movements the body may make. Instinct would persuade the average golfer to sit back into his heels in order to counteract the feelin of falling forward when playing the stroke. But the spinal posture which would result from such action would be quite upright, and that would cause the plane of the arc to be flat. How, then, can a flat arc get down to strike a ball that is below the level of the feet? It cannot.

It is necessary for the player to tilt the spine forward so that it may create an upright arc which will, when opposite, reach the low level of the ball. To achieve this, the front muscles of the thighs and shins must take the forward strain of the swing's movement.

The arc will steepen, but due to the limiting effect on the shoulder turn, will be very narrow. This player must accept, and settle for the fact that a more lofted club should be chosen in such circumstances and that the ball should be positioned back to centre.

Direction of Flight

When the sole of the club, together with the body's forward lean, is level with the slope, its face will be forced to send the ball to the right. This, together with a loss of distance, must be accepted and the player must allow for it by aiming off to the left of the target.

Standing above the ball is the most difficult of the 'sloping lies'. Only by balancing as far forward as he dare does the player gain a sufficient tilt of the spine to permit an upright swing-plane.

The combination of the up-and-down angle of the swing, which limits the turn of the shoulders, coupled with the fact that when the club's sole rests true to the slope it actually spins the ball 'off' line, is what sends the ball away to the right. This should be allowed for when aiming.

The player must decide whether the slope is gentle enough to permit a good attacking shot. The very steep hill requires that balance is secure, therefore he may have to 'sit back on his heels' a little more — take a more lofted club — then play safely for good position.

STANDING BELOW THE BALL

This is a much easier stroke, provided the golfer does not lean forward with his spine to gain 'natural' balance. (A forward spine creates a steep arc and that would cause the clubhead to 'go to earth' before it reached the ball.)

Sitting back, with weight towards the heels and the main strain taken up by the leg muscles just below the seat plus those of the calves, gives the spine the necessary uprightness to provide a shallow arc for the swing which keeps the clubhead 'above ground' until the ball is swept off.

The shallow swing will encourage a very full arc and shoulder turn with little awareness of hand action. The ball must therefore be positioned opposite a forward point. Very long clubs may be used from this lie and great distances covered, so there is always likely to be a totally inelegant finish with the body rolling, right shoulder over left.

With the sole of the club on the ground, the face will automatically send the ball to the left; the player should allow for this by aiming well to the right of the target.

When standing below the ball the player should attempt to sit back from the slope as far as balance will permit. This encourages the upright angle of the spine to shallow the arc which then sweeps the ball away without the club meeting the turf before the ball.

The full shoulder turn encouraged by the flat plane, together with the direction the clubface points when its sole rests true to the slope, results in the ball being turned away to the left. This must be allowed for when aiming.

It is possible, provided the hill is not too steep, to be quite adventurous and even a wooden club may be used for good distance. However, if the player risks this on rather difficult terrain he might easily hit the ground before the ball and get nowhere!

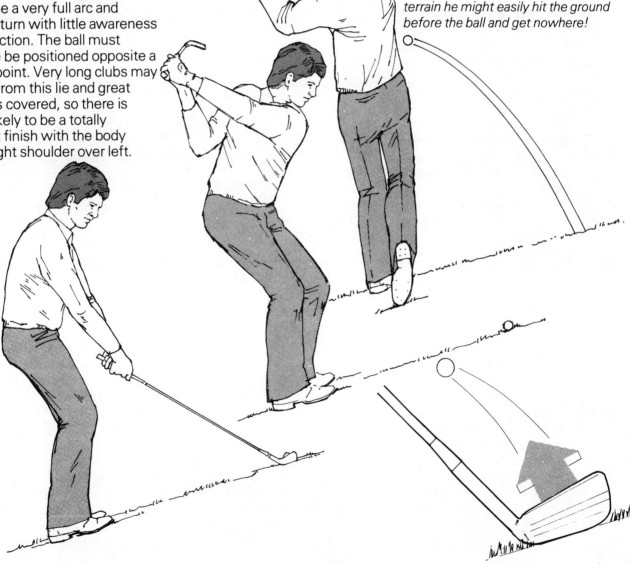

CHAPTER 21 — GOING DOWNHILL

The great difficulty with this shot, as opposed to going up a hill, is that the ground is higher than the ball on the immediate path of the clubhead towards it. The natural lean of the body, which would be back onto the back foot, would make it inevitable for the ground to be struck before the ball.

The body must be tilted with the slope, not against it, with the left knee taking more of the weight. A slight turning of the player's head to get his face parallel to the slope will also help, for that will bring the shoulder line also very close to parallel. In this way, the backswing will be immediately freed from contact with the ground but will be very upright.

The player must attempt to get the clubhead to swing 'down the slope' after it hits the ball, which is placed back in the stance. The descending blow is obviously going to subtract loft from the clubface and a low flight will result. Therefore, when a certain club would normally be chosen for a given yardage, a more lofted one could cover the same yardage when the downhill shot is played.

The danger when going down a slope, is that, should the body be positioned vertical to the horizon, the clubhead will strike the ground before contacting the ball and the shot will be completely fluffed.

The player must get his weight onto his left leg and his body vertical to the slope. The backswing will be rather steep as will the descent; however the ball can be positioned farther back to allow for this. The advantage is that the clubhead may swing freely on, as though going downhill parallel to the slope.

The trajectory of a ball hit from a piece of level ground will be lower than one hit, by the same club, when the slope is going upwards.

The player must select a straighter faced club i.e., a no. 4 instead of a no. 5 even though the total yardage to be covered would normally be done by the no. 5.

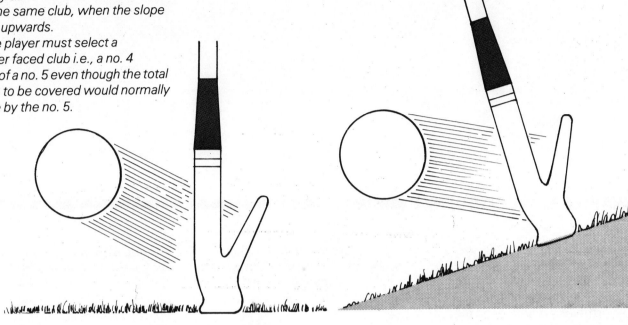

CHAPTER 22 — GOING UPHILL

Average players find this the easiest of the slopes simply because the chances of hitting ground before ball are removed; nevertheless many, even though they strike the ball, find a poor quality of flight. Often a smothered shot occurs: this happens when the body weight leans towards the upslope and the descent path of the swing, instead of being able to sweep up the hill with the slope, crushes the ball into the turf.

By leaning back towards the right knee, so that the shoulders become at least parallel with the upslope, the base of the arc may flow up the contour of the turf and so offer the full loft of the clubface to the ball. The club's loft will be exaggerated and the flight of the ball will be higher. A straighter-faced club than would be normal for the distance is therefore required.

No matter how the player attempts to lean back from the slope, there is an incentive to move forward, simply to get through; so the ball is positioned well forward in the stance. On occasions where the hill is not steep enough to warrant a 'recovery' stroke, the player may not be able to get the swing through and may find the body weight is stuck on that back leg. Should this happen, the ball, though it may be well struck and might well travel far, will be pulled away to the left. This should always be allowed for.

Playing up a gentle slope.
A player whose body is vertical to the horizon would drive clubhead and ball into the rise of the slope and probably smother it from gaining proper backspin. By leaning the body so that it gets close to being vertical from the slope, rather than the horizon, the club is allowed to swing through the ball without interference.

The right leg has to take the bodyweight and maintain it throughout the backswing preparation and, whilst this may limit the amount the body can turn, the path for the club to swing freely through is clear.

The trajectory of a ball hit from level ground will be higher than that, hit by the same club, when the ground clopes downhill. Therefore, where a no. 5 iron would be the choice for a certain distance, a no. 6 iron would cover a similar distance when being struck from a downhill lie.

SUMMING UP THE SLOPING LIES

If a player is prepared to sacrifice a bit of distance by arguing with Nature's tendency towards balance, then the clubhead can be given the opportunity to make a good connection with the ball.

While one may be a little adventurous from a slope when playing into an open space — for example, towards the fairway on a par 5 hole, where the green is out of range, anyway — he should steer clear of trying for too much power into a target area that might carry a lot of hazards, or even out-of-bounds problems. When the ball is not lying too well, it is often wiser to play for position than to risk all and end up with nothing.

CHAPTER 23 — BUNKER PLAY

In all problem strokes in golf, it is better to think first and apply common sense; and bunkers are no exception to this rule. Even more trouble is encountered here by the average golfer who attempts too much. It should be remembered that a bunker is a hazard strategically placed for the sole purpose of causing the player who has played the wrong line, chosen the wrong club or simply had a mishit, to pay a penalty.

The player who, by means of skill, escapes the penalty is the exception and certainly not the rule. So many golfers complain bitterly, if the ball is plugged a bit in soft sand close to the bunker-face and the only escape is sideways: with a long way yet to go, they have to settle for pitching the ball some 40 yards down the fairway. But it is the stroke that put them in there in the first place they should be criticising, not the hazard!

Basically, there are two types of bunker: the greenside bunker, of which there is normally an abundance (often as many as four or five surrounding a green); and the fairway bunkers, normally situated at the edges of the fairways. In the 'olden days' of golf-course design, the fairway bunkers lay right across the fairway like

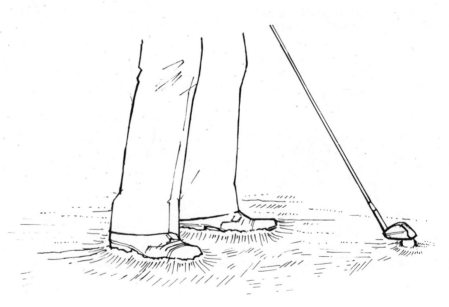

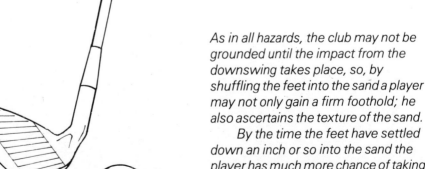

As in all hazards, the club may not be grounded until the impact from the downswing takes place, so, by shuffling the feet into the sand a player may not only gain a firm foothold; he also ascertains the texture of the sand.

By the time the feet have settled down an inch or so into the sand the player has much more chance of taking a good amount of sand with his stroke: after all, the full swing engaged in bunkers must not catch the ball clean — it could send it way over the green.

117

hurdles. Modern design is more likely to situate them on the shortest route of a 'dog-leg' hole, to catch the greedy player who wishes to shorten the hole.

Entirely different approaches are required for the two types of bunker. While a long bunker shot will never be played from a green side bunker, the greenside version of the shot must often be used from the fairway bunker, when the lie of the ball puts any achievement of distance out of the question.

The Greenside Bunker
THE SPLASH SHOT

If you are beginning to suspect that there is not, after all, just one golf swing — be reassured! The bunker shot is in fact an adaptation of a pitch shot. It simply engages extra percentage of some of the departments, while discarding

others. (This, by the way, is exactly how every trick shot in golf is played).

What is essential close to the green is to get plenty of height on to the flight of the ball, and at the same time develop a little forward thrust. To achieve this, the ball is actually cut across — rather like a cut-spin shot at table tennis, in which the bat travels down across the ball from *out-to-in*. (No excuse is made for introducing table tennis into a golf book, for people comprehend spin more readily when they think of a large hitting surface and a very light ball: it is only when the golf ball is thought of as a potential spinning object that the variety of strokes comes to a golfer).

If the shoulders refuse to turn in a swing but the hands and wrists add the percentage lost from the

shoulders *to that of their own,* then the club will travel up from the ball going outwards. If, at that point, the bottom half of the body were to lead through as normal, the club would be dragged from outwards across the ball to inwards across the body; and, because of the extra wrist action that took place going up, it would have an *open face.* That is the secret of the additional height gained when a ball is splashed from sand. (The term 'splash' is used to describe what happens when a light layer of sand is removed from under the ball, with the cutting edge of the open clubface requiring only a light swing. The amount of sand hit before contact is made could be measured as approximately one inch.)

The travelling of the blade of the very lofted sand iron across the

This is an ideal situation to play a splash *shot. The ball has to fly up sharply to get over the face to which it is fairly close: yet because the flag is not too far away a soft flight would be desired.*

By opening the stance and the shoulders, the swing path of the club will travel across the direct ball-to-target line — however the clubface is turned away from the line of the stance and aims at the flag, giving the impression of being open.

ball is a major factor in reducing the forward power of the blow. Another factor is the player's turning his body-line away from the target by taking up an open stance. Yet another 'weakener' is the ball's being played from a very forward position.

All these aids to the reduction of power permit the player to enlarge the arc to one that would, under normal circumstances, send the ball much too far. The extra length of the arc adds to the upward flight of the ball.

Once the ability to throw the ball up without sending it forward is mastered, only a variation in the speed of the swing is required to play very short shots or slightly longer ones. No long shot can be played from this swing and it would be wrong to force it.

. . . By maintaining the open clubface throughout the entire movement a 'splash' of sand may occur — scooping the sand before, under, and after the ball, so the ball floats upwards high yet softly.

The rather full, but rather slow swing which must be made, often causes the less experienced golfer to panic and, just before impact, he hurries the club into the sand.

It is necessary to swing through at one constant speed and to carry on as though the ball weighed nothing.

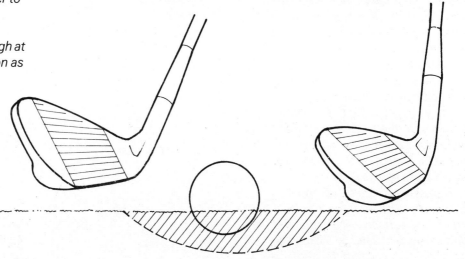

Chipping from greenside bunkers?
There is a great temptation, when the
ball lies very close to the green, to chip
the ball cleanly from the top surface of
sand, especially when the lie is good
and the bunker face is very low. After
all, why take the risk of the fuller swing
of the splash shot when there are only
a few feet to be covered? The answer
is simply this: the success rate of a
splash shot, in the case of an expert, is
about 90%; with a clean chip attempt
it would be as low as 60%.

The average high handicapper
who is likely to be tempted to chip
from the top surface will find that the
slightest touch of sand by the leading
edge of his club will turn the clubface
downward and the ball will remain in
the bunker.

*Nick Faldo holds the clubface open and
gains maximum elevation from the
face of the bunker.*

(Peter Dazeley)

PLUGGED BALL

The splash shot cannot be played when the ball has become buried in sand. The player may, however, use a fairly similar technique provided the stance is squared up a bit and the club head also. Too open a clubhead would prevent the necessary penetration to get to the sand beneath the plugged ball.

There is little hope of achieving the stop spin one sees from professionals playing the splash shot, for there is such a mass of sand between blade and ball from this lie. Allowance must be made, therefore, for the ball to run forward on landing.

The depth the ball is down and the texture of the sand must be taken into consideration when choosing the position of the ball, which cannot be played from the forward position of the splash shot. It must be brought back in the stance according to the severity of the lie; though only in the most desperate situation should it be behind the centre of the stance.

Such action makes following-through almost impossible — but one of the great secrets of success in bunker play is that the player sets out to achieve the impossible! So, even though as much as two or three inches of sand must be intentionally 'blasted' before the ball, an effort to get right through is essential.

A great deal of knowledge may be gained about the sand's texture by shuffling one's feet into the sand when taking up the stance. It is essential to get a good footing; and since the club is not allowed to make contact with the sand until the actual strike, 'shuffling' is the only permitted method of testing.

The Fairway Bunker

It is most unwise to attempt to gain a lot of distance, no matter how far away the green is, if the ball is lying badly or close to the face of the fairway bunker. In fact, even when the lie looks good it is good policy to select a club that has slightly more loft than the club with which one

'might just make it' over the top. This is because, should the leading edge of the blade contact sand — even just a little — before the ball, it will drive itself down, causing the clubface to deloft; and the flight of the ball would then be low enough to hit the bunker rim.

The grip used is the normal one, except that the hands should be down the handle a little. This is advisable as a means of compensation for the change of ground level when the feet have shuffled into the sand for their firm foothold.

The ball should be positioned opposite the centre of the feet to avoid sand being contacted before the ball.

Then, with a feeling of chin-up — another way of avoiding a heavy contact — the normal golf swing is engaged. While expert golfers may be seen playing very long irons, sometimes even wooden clubs, the average player would be well-advised to use nothing less lofted than a middle iron.

CHAPTER 24 — RECOVERY STROKES

There are many great players who are renowned as recovery players: usually those with the most competitive natures, who never give up trying and so get the best results possible. Players with a defeatist attitude are normally poor at recovery strokes, for their mood of depression over whatever it is they must recover from dims the concentration required to adapt.

A recovery stroke may often be a complete original, a trick shot, even; however, once a clear knowledge of the various departments of the swing has been acquired, it is quite surprising just what may be accomplished. The essence of the recovery shot is that it must achieve just that! No attempt should be made which might move the ball 'from the frying pan into the fire'. Often, the dropping of a stroke must be accepted and a safe route to the green be chosen. Determination to succeed and heroics are not the same thing!

The essential factor is that the cleanest hit at the ball possible must be achieved. Should the ball lie in thick grass or on such a slope that balance is difficult to maintain, then a loften club must be used, even though it may limit the achievable distance.

Thick Rough

The normal golf grip is sufficiently strong to remove the ball from the worst of lies. Novices, however, are inclined to grip with the palm of the right hand in search of greater strength. It is a good plan to go down the handle a little, since the resulting tilt forward of the spine causes a more upright plane and this helps with getting down to the ball.

The ball must be played further back in the stance, midway between centre and the right foot, thereby eliminating a lot of the grass, which could be swept forward ahead of the blade and so dull the connection.

The stance and aim of the body should be square to the direction desired, not open as in the case of greenside bunkers shots; for, although a good lift may be required, a solid hit is a feature of this shot.

To achieve the cleanest possible connection with the ball, certain adjustments must be made from the orthodox swing. By combining the 'back' ball position with a reduction of shoulder turn, the hands and arms are committed to a fairly sharp lift in the backswing preparation which makes possible the required downward blow.

Clearly, such an attack would tend to reduce the actual loft of the clubface and it is therefore necessary to use a very lofted club.

The de-lofting causes the ball to fly on a lower-than-normal trajectory, which is an advantage when the player is attempting to make as much yardage as possible towards a distant green. On the occasion when the green is within reach, it must be borne in mind that, however upright the swing may be made, grass will always get between blade and ball, eliminating any chance of backspin; so there must be allowance for forward run. Should a bunker lie between player and flag, another route to the green should be considered; for the ball that carries the bunker must surely overshoot the green.

Severe Slopes

The majority of severe slopes are encountered where the ball has missed the green and a difficult approach is to be made. In such cases it is often necessary to place great stress on balancing the body by leaning against the hill, which requires the shots to be played virtually by hands, wrists and arms only.

Going up a steep bank is the easiest of the severe slopes for, even though the body weight is leaning into the hill, there is nothing to impede a clean hit at the ball, which must be positioned well-forward even outside the left foot. However, unlike the case of sweeping up a gentle slope, the club is going to chop into the bank immediately after contact with the ball, so a very lofted club must be used — even a sand iron.

From the sharp chop, done mainly with the hands and wrists, the ball will pop up at quite a sharp angle. It is more the steepness of its climb which makes it stop reasonably quickly, rather than backspin.

In extreme circumstances the player may have to place the hands well down the shaft, even to the extent of going off the end of the grip. In many 'short shots' such as this, a 'short club' is a great asset

A severe uphill requires the player to secure his balance so, unlike the gentle slope rule, he gets the body vertical to the horizon.

In order to get a fairly good distance from the stroke the backswing should set off swinging almost down-hill. Then a distinct feeling of pulling the club uphill through the ball will get the best from the poor lie.

If the slope is desperately steep then a very lofted club, such as a Sand Iron, should be used for the club will chop into the ball: without sufficient loft on the blade the ball could be buried into the bank.

and gives a feeling of control.

Going down a steep slope is a very difficult shot: since the player is committed to leaning into the slope, he is increasing the likelihood of striking the ground before reaching the ball.

A very lofted club should be used here, because the downward blow will de-loft the club.

The ball must be positioned well back, even outside the right foot, and the club should be held well down the handle.

There is no chance whatsoever of gaining any

backspin and a great deal of run-out should be allowed for. A shot played from a grassy bank down onto a green will simply 'scamper' across it.

Going along a slope with the ball below the level of the feet requires the player to sit well back

Going down a steep slope promotes great problems. The player must get his body vertical to the horizon in order to keep balance, and doing so makes it difficult to keep the blade from 'grounding' before contact is made with the ball.

The ball should be positioned way back even though that may be well behind the stance: a rapid wrist action should be used which will cause an up then down chopping action. Each of these require that a club with a great deal of loft be used.

into the hill for good balance, so it becomes difficult to reach the ball. Much 'sitting down' has to be done and a very up and down strike, made by a sharp hand-and-wrist action, is applied.

The ball should be positioned opposite the centre of the stance and a lofted club, gripped at full length, used in the hope of a clean hit.

No attempt should be made to gain great distance, for there is every likelihood that the ball will be hit near the socket of the club. Even when contacted safely in the blade, the flight of the ball, as a result of the steep action, will be off to the right.

Standing well below the level of the ball on a bank makes it awkward to know where to put the handle of the club, which appears to be prodding into the stomach.

The secret is to position the ball forward and then, by gripping well down the handle, have the excess of grip protruding beyond the left hip. Because there will be a rather sharp hand-and-wrist action, the extra bit of handle will always

be to the left of the body. One advantage of this shot is that it will have a low, strong, hooking flight, which makes quite a bit of distance obtainable. However, if the bank is close to the green, then run must be allowed for.

SUMMING UP
Golf is played over three or four miles of often quite rugged terrain and many varieties of trouble shot are therefore encountered beyond simply being on one kind of slope or another. As long as certain facts are understood, however, even the most humble golfer may produce a recovery shot to equal that of one of his golfing idols.
The basic facts are these:
HIGH FLIGHT
By limiting the body work and increasing the hand-and-wrist work, height is put on to the ball's flight.
LOW FLIGHT
By stifling the hand-and-wrist and increasing the arm and shoulder turn, a low trajectory is created.
HIGH FLIGHT
By putting the ball forward in the stance and opening the blade,

greater lift is available and backspin is created.
LOW FLIGHT
By positioning the ball back in the stance and closing the blade, the ball may be driven forward and 'run' made available.
HIGH FLIGHT
By narrowing the stance, one creates greater emphasis on hand, wrist and arm-swinging which makes the swing go upright and so adds height — and a bit of slice spin — to the flight.
LOW FLIGHT
By widening the stance, a stiffening of the forearms and a flattening of the arc is brought about. The resulting scythe-like action drives in overspin, which makes the ball fly low and run.
HIGH FLIGHT
By gripping the full length of a club, when only a short distance is being covered, though a very risky method, a softer height of flight occurs.
LOW FLIGHT
By going down the handle a long way, a bracing of the forearms and wrists occurs which can be used to drive a ball forwards.

PART FIVE — FAULT-FINDING AND CORRECTION; SHAPING SHOTS

CHAPTER 25 — THE APPROACH

Golf is a very difficult game to play really well, and consequently only a handful of players have achieved the stature of being described as 'great' players. However there are lots of 'good' players, and even more not-so-good ones, who derive a great deal of pleasure from the game: golf's handicap system, which attempts to 'make all men equal', has seen to that.

At one time or another, even the best of players run into difficulties and acquires a flaw in the swing. Such a fault must, however, be diagnosed quickly and accurately, and then disposed of before it causes permanent

damage to the muscle-memory of the swing — and, of course, to the player's confidence.

There are many good golfers who actually live with a fault built into their swing. The original cause of the fault may have been either physical or mental; the important point is that it has been compensated for consistently. It should be remembered that, though the orthodox swing is normally the one that suits the physique of the person using it this should not be taken to mean that tall strong men will inevitably do better than those of smaller stature.

Happily, history has shown this not to be the case. There have been as many great little players as there have been large. Ben Hogan of the United States was described as the greatest ever, though only a little over 5½ feet; Gary Player of South Africa is another; and at a similar height there is Lee Trevino, who is the master of adapting his swing to play all sorts of strokes. There have been players, too, who have risen above deformity: Ed Furgol had a withered arm, yet he won the United States Open Championship; and Vicente Fernandez whose right leg is shorter than his left owing to a childhood accident, is a consistent tournament winner. These people developed their swings around what was available to create a competitive game to match the world's best players.

What has to be sought by the beginner is the orthodox golf swing described in detail in Parts 2 and 3 of this book. If the guide lines of orthodoxy were followed exactly, then of course the ball would fly straight and always land in the middle of the fairway; irons shots would be in the centre of the green; and all putts would go in. However, that is very unlikely to happen! So, when the ball flies crooked and comes down off the fairway, or when the greens are missed and bunker shots have to be played all too frequently — the fault causing the problem must be located and put right.

The simplest means of getting to the bottom of things quickly is to have a set of guide lines from which to work. There is no point in guessing at causes: attempting to remedy the wrong 'cause' might well damage the swing still further. The sequence in which this book has detailed the construction of the swing is exactly the sequence in which you should seek the cause of any fault. Familiarity with that 'sequence' is your first advantage.

Your second advantage should be a clear understanding of the various flights the ball might perform and into which group they come. This is the point at which many golfers become confused: they cannot see how one shot that finishes away to the left can be in the same family as one that curves off to the right. These groups are therefore shown in the form of a graph, which clearly shows how the direction on which the clubhead travels is that which

initiates the take-off direction of the ball. After those first yards, according to the spin applied, the ball may change and curve in exactly the opposite direction.

Many good golfers prefer a shape of flight other than straight! This is less strange than it may sound, in fact. A ball that is sent off in the hope of a straight flight could fall away either to the left or to the right, so the player has both sides of the fairway to worry about. On the other hand, the player who *deliberately* applies a spin commits the ball to travel to only one side of the fairway and can eliminate the problem of hazards, etc., on the opposite side of the hole.

It is not intended that this be seen as an excuse for accepting a bad shot in the belief that, provided it goes the same way all the time, it is all right. It is not! The type of spin referred to is a very mild form indeed and furthermore is deliberately applied by the experienced player, who only applies a spin that is both suited to his physique and calculated to give the best result.

Those three celebrated men mentioned earlier all set out, in defiance of their lack of height, to attain the widest arc they could physically make. This stretching, being on the flat plane of a small person, tended to cause a hook flight (in which the ball curves from left to right). All three had developed a lot of power, however, and fortunately each was of sufficiently determined character to combat the odd damaging hook that occured when things were overdone. In time, both Hogan (who no longer competes but who contributed so much to our knowledge of the golf swing) and Trevino sacrificed the yardage gained by the *hook-spin* by

converting to *'fading'* the ball, which is a deliberately induced mild form of slice. This stroke carries more control and is applied by those competitors who normally hit huge distances and who therefore can sacrifice a little power for greater control. The third man mentioned, Gary Player, though now in his 40's, has not given up the search for power. He still stretches his swing to the limit and so, now and again, gets an odd violent hook for which he is in continual search of a cure.

Good Fault — Bad Fault
It would be much better that the average player develops a swing that, when it fails to hit the ball straight, sends it with a hook-spin — *never* with a slice-spin. This policy could apply to the big player, too; for, while many tall professionals apply a fade-spin, they are all converting to that from a swing developed originally on hook-spin lines.

Why 'Hook'-Spin?
If one could look down from a high platform onto a golfer swinging a driver, one would see an arc curving around the player. If one then imagined the player's arms and club performing continuous circles, it would be understood that anything flying from such a circle must curve as if an extension of that circle — *and a hook would be the natural extension*. While up on that platform, one would also understand clearly why the smaller player, whose arc is shallow, would encourage a greater hook-spin. On the other hand, the arc made by a very tall man would be more upright and would give a milder spin-off.

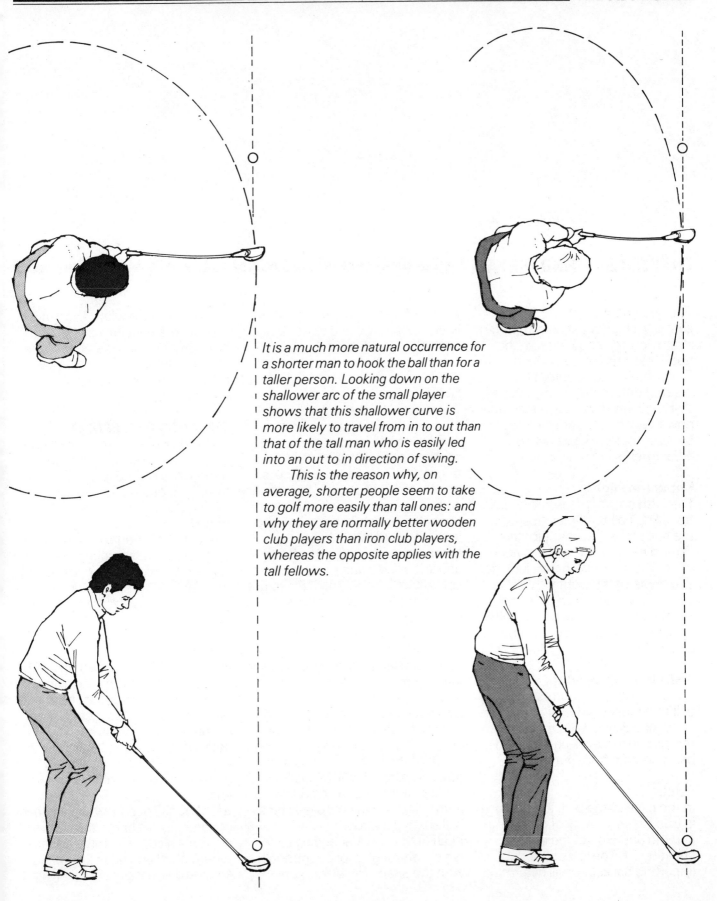

It is a much more natural occurrence for a shorter man to hook the ball than for a taller person. Looking down on the shallower arc of the small player shows that this shallower curve is more likely to travel from in to out than that of the tall man who is easily led into an out to in direction of swing.

This is the reason why, on average, shorter people seem to take to golf more easily than tall ones: and why they are normally better wooden club players than iron club players, whereas the opposite applies with the tall fellows.

CHAPTER 26 — FIND THE FAULT

The search for whatever flaw is causing a fault must be completed in the correct 'sequence', in the hope that it may be found early in it. Fortunately, most faults are created before the swing actually starts moving; and it is remarkable how many mishits are eliminated by the simplest of pre-swing adjustments.

Know the Flights
The path on which the clubhead is travelling has the first influence on the ball and will account for the initial direction covered, provided the ball is struck with the clubface. The angle of the clubface will impart any spin which, after the initial journey, will cause the ball to turn, be it upwards, downwards or sideways.

THE OUT-TO-IN FAMILY
Pull and Slice, although sending the ball to opposite sides of the target, are in one group, with the path of the clubhead travelling across the ball at impact from *out* to *in*.

PULL
In the case of the pull, the clubface is true to the journey of the swing and the direction of the ball is straight left. The loft of the club, imparting backspin, will determine the height of the flight but this is likely to be low since *out*-to-*in* normally provides a descending blow.

SLICE
The journey of the clubhead in a slice shot is (just as in pulling) across the ball from *out* to *in*, which sets the ball off to the left of the target. However, the clubface is open from that journey and causes an *out*-to-*in* side-spin, which turns the ball from left to right *after* the initial forward thrust has completed. The ball sets off low and left, then soars upward and spins away to the right of the target in one of the weakest flights the ball can make.

In the same group as pull and slice come *skying* and *fluffing,* for all are caused by a club descending into the ball from too steep an angle.
SKYING occurs normally during a tee-shot with a wood, when the club descends so steeply that too much of the clubface loft is turned downwards; the ball overlaps onto the top of the clubhead and an artificial backspin is applied and the ball soars upwards.
FLUFFING is a descending blow which, although more common with the sharp iron blade, can happen with any club. The turf is met before the club catches the ball and rises between them: the amount of turf determines how badly the forward flight of the ball is weakened.

THE IN-TO-OUT FAMILY
Push and Hook also commit the ball to opposite sides of the target; though the clubhead's journey is from *in* to *out* in both cases.

PUSH
The ball is pushed when the clubhead travels through the hitting area on a direction of in to out with the clubface true to that journey, and the ball travels straight to the right.

HOOK
Hook has the ball curving away to the left, occurs when the clubhead travels (as with the push) from in to out but has the club face rolling closed from that journey. The ball sets off to the right, then the in-to-out side-spin turns it, normally in quite a powerful flight, away to the left.
SHANKING occurs when, instead of catching the ball in the centre of an iron's blade, the ball is struck where shaft and head are joined and the ball 'shoots off' to the right.

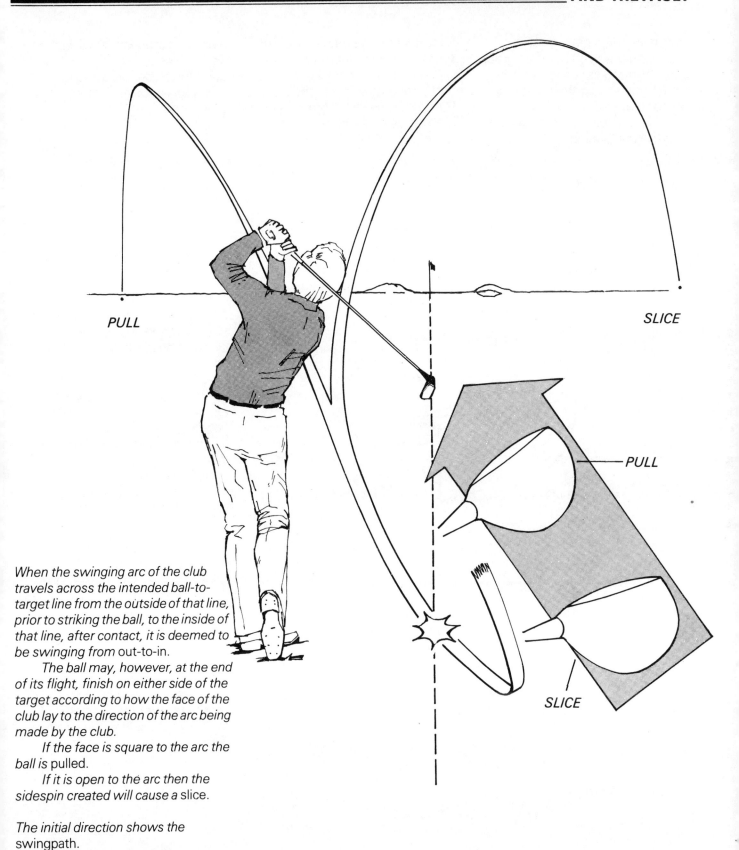

PULL

SLICE

PULL

SLICE

When the swinging arc of the club travels across the intended ball-to-target line from the outside of that line, prior to striking the ball, to the inside of that line, after contact, it is deemed to be swinging from out-to-in.

The ball may, however, at the end of its flight, finish on either side of the target according to how the face of the club lay to the direction of the arc being made by the club.

If the face is square to the arc the ball is pulled.

If it is open to the arc then the sidespin created will cause a slice.

The initial direction shows the swingpath.
The secondary direction, if any, the angle of face.

Unfortunately, many golfers associate this with the slice group; and efforts to cure slice lead to disaster in shank, the most dreaded of golf's bad shots.

The real cause of shanking is that the backswing is on too flat a plane and the resulting in-to-out direction of the clubhead towards the ball brings the socket of the club outwards to meet the ball. **TOPPING,** another common fault in golf, has no set group — it belongs to all of them. The clubhead strikes the ball high on its circumference so that, instead of spinning backwards and thus up, it spins forwards and attempts to go down into the ground.

SKYING and *FLUFFING* are part of the out-to-in family where the arc of the club descends too steeply towards the ball.

The shallow head of the wood allows part of the ball to pass over the top which creates a false, weak backspin. It also badly damages the paintwork, leaving a tell-tale trade mark.

The sharp leading edge of an iron penetrates the ground before contacting the ball, raising a cushion of grass and earth which defuses all power from the strike.

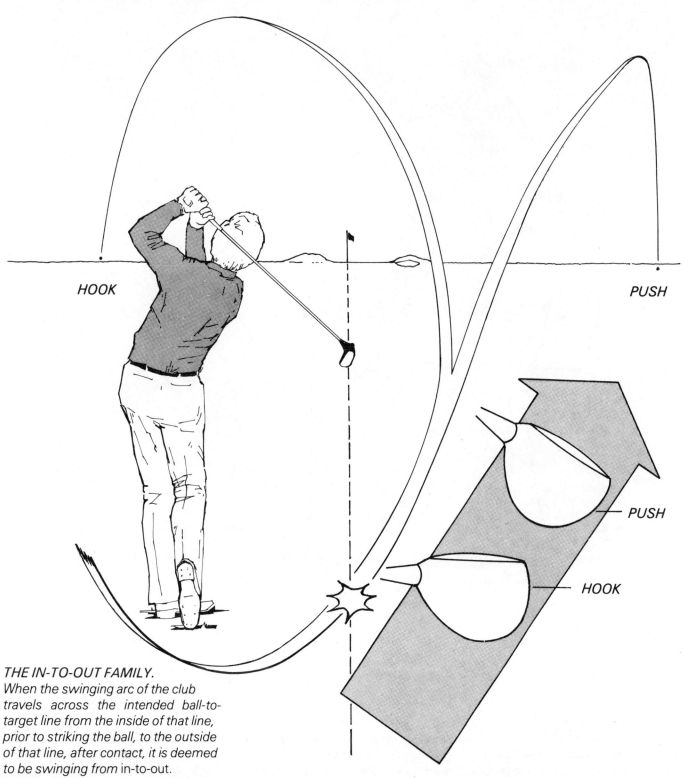

HOOK

PUSH

PUSH

HOOK

THE IN-TO-OUT FAMILY.

When the swinging arc of the club travels across the intended ball-to-target line from the inside of that line, prior to striking the ball, to the outside of that line, after contact, it is deemed to be swinging from in-to-out.

The ball may, however, at the end of its flight, finish on either side of the target according to how the face of the club lay to the direction of the arc being made by the club.

If the face is square to the arc the ball is pushed.

If it is open to the arc then the sidespin created will cause a hook.

The initial direction shows the swingpath.

The secondary direction, if any, the angle of face.

133

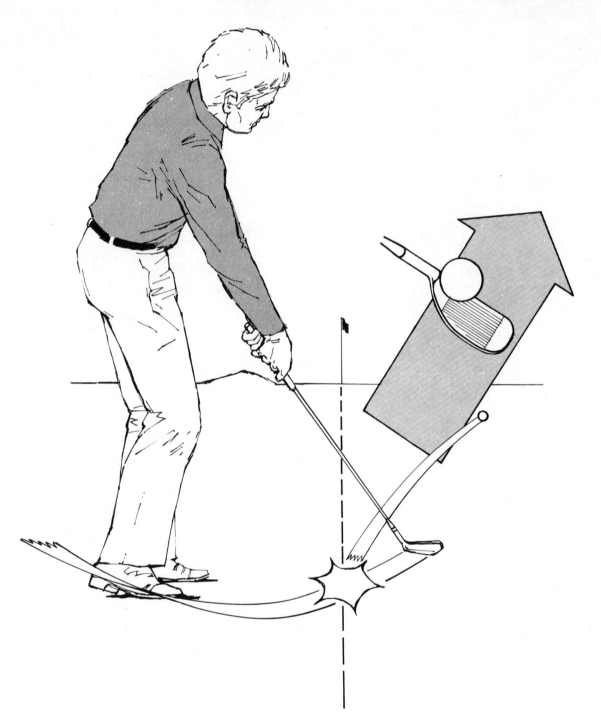

SHANKING

The shot in golf which many good players refuse to discuss because they believe it has infectious qualities. Any club member who is prone to it is thought of as a 'carrier' and may be shunned.

The reason for all of this is that the direction the ball flies conveys the very opposite meaning to the player. Because it flies to the right it resembles a slice, which is a member of the out-to in family. The sufferer then attempts to adjust his swing for a hooking flight from the in-to-out family. He is then in the hands of the 'disease' for the shank is in-to-out!

The swing path has become so inside to outside that it causes the arc's plane to flatten and the pushing through effect sends the socket of the club towards the ball.

Only by attempting to swing on a more upright plane and slightly outside-to-in will a cure be effected.

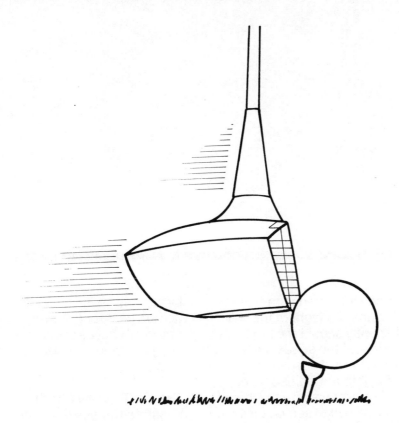

The *TOPPED* shot belongs to no set family and can happen to anyone, although most common amongst inexperienced players, particularly on the opening holes of a round before the 'eye' is in and the muscles are free. It is surprising how a few minutes on a practice ground or in a net can eliminate these early tops.

CHAPTER 27 — THE CURE SEQUENCE

When a golfer slips into one of the game's faults, he — or she — becomes prey to all those would-be teachers of the game, many of whom possess a variety of theories which would confuse most properly trained teaching professionals. Advice from the unqualified should be avoided at all costs, for it may cause long-lasting damage. Mentors of this kind frequently search for the most complicated means of curing what is a simple basic fault; and, most damningly, fail to work their diagnosis step-by-step through the sequence on which a swing is founded.

The first thing a player should do when confronted by a consistently misdirected shot is establish, if necessary with the help of the direction-of-flight graph in this book, to which family group the fault belongs. Then, by consulting the following lists (given under the appropriate headings) set about checking each item listed, from 1 to 9. With luck, the fault may be detected very early in the list. If it is, the correction necessary to re-establish the orthodox position or movement should be made — and given the opportunity to eliminate the bad habit that has taken its place. Only

if those steps do not improve the swing and the flight of the ball sufficiently should the next numbers of the sequence be checked and, if suspect, the appropriate remedies applied.

The professional teacher of golf is trained to search for swing faults with an eye that checks (within the time it takes the golfer to hit as few as two or three balls) right through the same sequence on which he builds swings into beginners. And his brother professional who plays on the tournament circuits shows that same sequence going into operation every time he prepares, then hits, a ball. So a frustrated golf sufferer, after months of fruitless searching, may find his cure revealed in 'the wink of an eye' — but only of an experienced eye! Here is the sequence in which the fault should be sought:

1. Clubface
2. Hands
3. Ball position
4. Stance
5. Line-Up
6. Posture
7. Backswing
8. Downswing
9. Throughswing

Most of golf's faults are to be found between numbers 1 and 6, for it is

before the swing starts that most golfers go wrong. Nevertheless, potential causes of particular faults are given below for each of the nine areas.

THE OUT-TO-IN FAMILY
Possible Causes of a Pull

1. **Clubface** The clubface is not normally at fault.
2. **Hands** The hands may both be turned to the player's right, i.e., left hand showing more than two knuckle joints, with the vee between right forefinger and thumb pointing to player's right shoulder.
3. **Ball position** The ball may be too far forward.
4. **Stance** The stance may be too narrow, giving shoulders the initiative in the downswing.
5. **Line-Up** The line-up of the feet may be closed (aiming off to the right), which results in the shoulders twisting open to compensate (off to the left).
6. **Posture** The posture may be leaning too far forward, especially if the ball is too far away.
7. **Backswing** The backswing prepares by picking the club upwards and outwards.
8. **Downswing** The downswing is from *out* travelling to *in*.

9. **Throughswing** The arms, drawn across the body by the *out*-to-*in* path, finish hugged in to the chest.

Possible Causes of a Slice

1. **Clubface** The clubface may lie open.
2. **Hands** The left hand may show less than two knuckle joints, and the right hand, quick to take advantage of this weakness, may climb over on top with its vee pointing at the player's left shoulder. This is known as a weak grip.
3. **Ball position** The ball is positioned too far forward in the stance.
4. **Stance** The stance itself may be narrow.
5. **Line-Up** The line-up of the feet may be open but the shoulders will definitely be open, i.e., pointing off to the left of target.
6. **Posture** The posture could be tilted through over-reaching for the ball.
7. **Backswing** The backswing may start either too much inwards, which causes the arc to lift up-and-out as a secondary stage; on the other hand it could be picking up directly outwards.
8. **Downswing** Whatever way it chooses to go up, the swing starts down from an outward position, travelling down and across the ball.
9. **Throughswing** The throughswing will be unbalanced, for travelling across the ball with the clubface open drives the player towards the back foot.

Possible Causes of Skying and Fluffing

The cause for either of these might be exactly as for either pull or slice but would depend on, in the case of skying, whether the club contacts the ball before entering the ground; or, in the case of fluffing, whether it contacts the ground before reaching the ball. Both shots are created when the journey of the clubhead towards the ball is too steep.

THE IN-TO-OUT FAMILY
Possible Causes of a Push

1. **Clubface** The clubface is not normally at fault.
2. **Hands** The hands may be a little *weak* in their position, with not quite two knuckles showing on the left hand: however, this is not normally a grip fault.
3. **Ball position** The ball position may be too far back, causing the swing to start too much on the *inside*.
4. **Stance** The stance may be too wide, so preventing the player from transferring his weight through to the finish.
5. **Line-Up** Line-up could be a little bit closed, with both feet and shoulders aiming off to the right.
6. **Posture** The posture could have the player sitting back on his heels, so causing a flat plane-of-swing.
7. **Backswing** The backswing is definitely on the inward direction too soon.
8. **Downswing** The hips lead too soon in the downswing causing the arc of the club to flatten and come even more from *in* to *out*.
9. **Throughswing** There is no recovery from the in-to-out delivery and the clubhead travels away to the right, following the flight of the ball.

Possible Causes of a Hook

1. **Clubface** The clubface could be well closed.
2. **Hands** One or both hands may be 'under' the handle, so that more than two knuckle joints of the left hand are visible to the player and the vee of the right forefinger and thumb is pointing away to his right. (This is known as a *strong grip*.)
3. **Ball position** The ball may be positioned opposite a point far back in the stance, which will drive the backswing tightly inwards.
4. **Stance** The stance may be too wide, forcing a lot of activity into the upper body movements.
5. **Line-Up** The line-up may have shoulders closed (pointing away to the right).
6. **Posture** The posture may be reduced in height, owing to the wide aggressive stance, yet the spine might be quite upright and causing flat arc to occur.
7. **Backswing** The backswing may be well on the inside, giving a great deal of shoulder turn.
8. **Downswing** The downswing travels towards the ball well from the inside but with the hands rolling the clubface closed in an effort to turn the ball back to the target.
9. **Throughswing** The finish is normally strong, for the hook is the powerful stroke; however, the right shoulder is often pulled up and over to finish in a high, ugly position.

Possible Causes of a Shank

1. **Clubface** The clubface may be laid a bit open in search of extra lift.
2. **Hands** The hands may be in the *weak* position with too few knuckles visible on the left hand.
3. **Ball position** The ball may be positioned too far back in the stance.
4. **Stance** The width of the stance is not normally a cause of shanking.
5. **Line-Up** The player may well have feet and shoulders aiming off to the left.
6. **Posture** The posture usually found is where the player sits back on the heels, bringing the spine nearly vertical and so causing a very flat take-away of the club.

This is the swing when true to the player's natural swing-plane. He is likely to return his swingpath true to the target line, with the clubface square.

7. **Backswing** The backswing is very much on the inside and in addition there may be a rolling of the wrist joints, which causes the clubface to turn open. The angle of the plane created by this movement becomes extremely

Elementary SLICE faults may well cause the club to change direction so that it is outside the player's natural swing-plane. He is then likely to swing across the ball with the clubface open.

flat.

8. **Downswing** The natural return of the hips and legs finds *them* leading the club from in to out, with the back of the left hand, which rolled, having no time to recover but leading the socket towards the ball.

9. **Throughswing** There is an ugly loss of balance, often resulting in the player having to step forward with the right foot, which tends to follow the outward journey of the clubhead.

Players who shank with regularity do, in fact, hook their better iron shots. There is a very fine line between recovering the clubface, which becomes the hook, and not quite making it, which becomes the shank.

Elementary HOOK faults will cause the club to change direction so that it is inside *the player's natural swing-plane. He is then likely to swing towards the ball from well* inside *with the clubface* closed.

Possible Causes of the Top

1. **Clubface** The clubface would be normal.
2. **Hands** The hands may be too tight which would delay proper hand action and cause the body to lift in the backswing.
3. **Ball position** Ball position may be too far forward, maybe even outside the left foot.
4. **Stance** Too wide a stance could stop the proper transfer of weight, leaving the body stranded on the back foot.
5. **Line-Up** Line-up is not normally a cause.
6. **Posture** Spine too erect may cause so flat a swing-plane that the ball would be missed.
7. **Backswing** The backswing, under tension (a beginner's fault), inhibits the free wrist movement required to get the feel through the shot.
8. **Downswing** There may be no transfer through with the body weight due to lack of confidence.
9. **Throughswing** The player who tops is usually found falling back, with eyes that were off the ball too early now searching the sky for a ball that isn't there.

There are some who hit it down! Eddie Polland, the Irish professional, strikes firmly down and through and shows a perfect example of head position . . .

(Bert Neale)

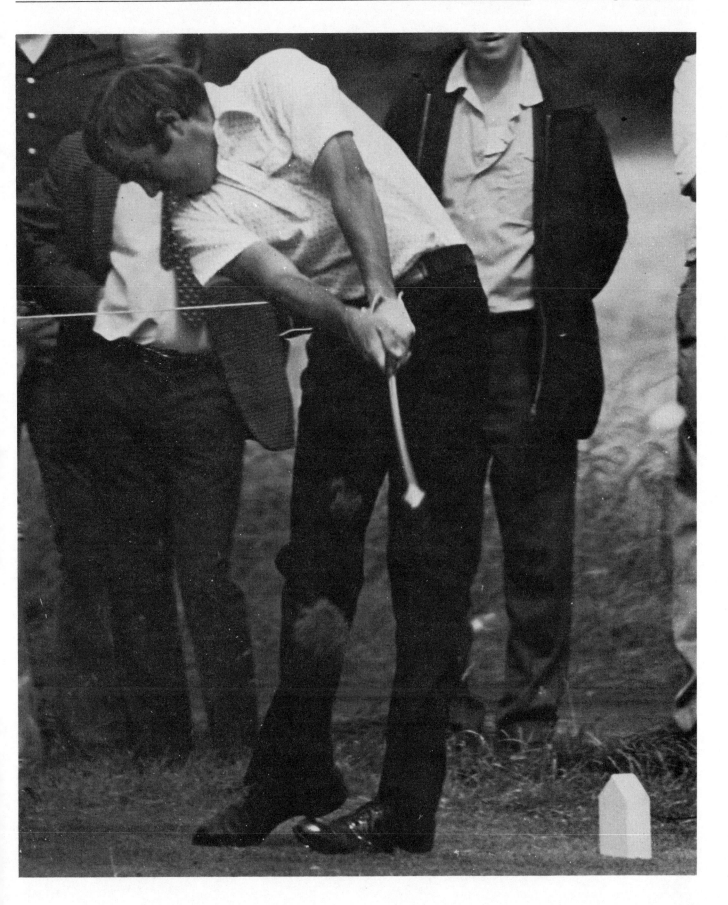

CHAPTER 28 — SHAPING SHOTS

Though this chapter is aimed at correction, the information is also ideal for the *deliberate creation* of faults. On many occasions in golfing, it becomes necessary to hit a crooked shot or some other form of trick shot in order to make the best of a difficult situation. This is a feature of the play of top golfers, whose ability to manufacture a required shot saves them many strokes on their score.

It is not only for the expert to play these shots. The most average of golfers, armed with a good knowledge of *the flights of the ball* and the *sequence,* may do quite extraordinary things with the ball. Remember that a skilful trick shot is achieved only through the deliberate application of a fault or faults.

The Choice

Unlike the unintended crooked shot, which produces variations no player would deliberately attempt whatever the situation, there is only a limited variety of trickshots that can safely be played deliberately.

From the *out-to-in* family, only forms of *slicing* the ball would be attempted. Pulling is itself a straight flight, which the player can create simply by aiming; while skying and fluffing are impossible to judge and therefore never attempted.

From the *in-to-out* family, the choice is confined to forms of *hooking.* Pushing is straight and could be aimed for; and shank would never be attempted under any circumstances.

There are those who hit it up! The incredible ability to swing up and through is what gives Severiano Ballesteros of Spain the ability to get up and over the highest of obstacles. He used this ability to help him win the British Open Championship and the American Masters within the same 12 months.

(Peter Dazeley)

CHAPTER 29 — WHEN AND HOW TO APPLY FORMS OF SLICE

When?

The full slice could be used to curve a ball around an obstacle, normally in the hope of getting towards the entrance to a green, rather than onto the green itself, for there is never great accuracy with the adventurous spin shots.

Fade could be applied with much greater finesse where there are, say, a lot of bunkers (even out of bounds), to the left of the green. The fade-spin would give the player a greater feeling of confidence, knowing that the spin he applies is taking the ball away from trouble. There is also the knowledge that the cutting-across spin of a fade weakens the flight of a ball, so it would stop more abruptly when landing. This would suit the golfer who fears overshooting his intended target.

How?

By studying the sequence that determines the causes of slice fault, a player can learn to apply the appropriate 'cause' to create a degree of slice spin. The violence of the slice depends on how far down the list the player selects the 'cause'. If the circumstances really seem to demand a desperate effort, however, it might be advisable to think of playing safely towards the open fairway.

SEQUENCE

1. **Clubface** By laying the clubface just a little open, one automatically creates a cutting spin. A point worth remembering is that it is easier for clubs with only a little loft to create side-spins. The additional loft of the steeper clubs imparts a degree of backspin that is often stronger than the amount of side-spin being applied. (This is why players prone to slicing with the driver hit much straighter shots when they resort to driving with a lofted wood, or even an iron club.)

2. **Hands** The grip should be slightly weakened by the knuckle joints visible on the left hand reducing from two to one, and the right coming over very slightly. (This type of grip is favoured by many strong professional golfers, particularly those who prefer a slight fade on all their strokes.)

3. **Ball position** Ball position would have to be a little further forward than for normal shots. (This allows the hips to get well out of the way on the downswing, and so permits the clubhead to travel across the ball.)

4. **Stance** The feet would be slightly closer together. (A narrow stance encourages more active hand action, which is a feature of slice shots.)

5. **Line-Up** The feet and hips would be aimed off to a point left of the intended target.

6. **Posture** There would be a definite turning of the shoulders off to the left of the target. (The path of a swing is dictated by the shoulder; open shoulders would lead the clubhead across the ball.) The left shoulder would be lower than in normal shots.

7. **Backswing** The hand-and-wrist action would work at a faster rate than the arms and shoulders and would accomplish their maximum preparation ahead of the others. (This is called 'having an open face' when the club reaches the top of the backswing, for the leading edge of the blade is no longer in line with the back of the forearm, as it is at set-up.)

8. **Downswing** This brings the clubhead down and across the ball, drawing the clubface right across it and so imparting the slice-spin.

9. **Throughswing** There is a distinct feeling of 'drawing across the ball' and the hands

lead the clubhead well through into the finish, never allowing the clubface to turn inwards.

It is hoped that no reader would attempt to apply all of these ingredients. They are given to allow the impression of cutting across the ball to be 'felt' into the swing.

What it boils down to is that there is a distinct increase in the percentage of certain of the swing's 'departments' (covered in the section on Swingbuilding) while at the same time, there is a quietening down of others. The hands and wrists, together with the feet and ankles, are definitely busier, while the arms and shoulders do much less. In this way a narrower arc is made, which brings the clubhead across the ball; and with the clubface adjusted to be open, a slice spin must happen.

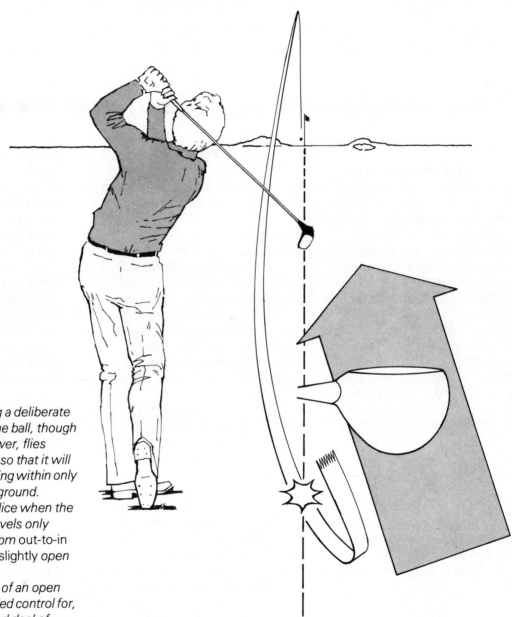

FADE SHOT.
The advantage of playing a deliberate fade is that of control. The ball, though slightly weakened in power, flies higher and lands gentler so that it will almost certainly stop rolling within only a few feet of hitting the ground.

It is a mild form of slice when the swing-path of the arc travels only slightly across the ball from out-to-in and the clubface is kept slightly open from that path.

It is the maintaining of an open face which gives the added control for, though it takes out a good deal of power, it dulls the more inaccurate aggression of the hands and wrists in the hitting area.

CHAPTER 30 — WHEN AND HOW TO APPLY FORMS OF HOOKING

When?

The full hook should be used as a recovery shot only when there is a need to turn it in flight around an obstacle. There is always great lack of control with this shot and it should never be attempted if a lot of trouble lies close to the intended target; much better to play a less ambitious shot into a more sensible spot.

Draw is very much a controlled shot and therefore one that may be played with accuracy. It is ideal for holding a ball up against a left-to-right cross-wind: it allows the player to aim straight at the target — the draw spin counteracts the cross-wind and the ball flies straight.

The draw flight is favoured by many, as the ideal flight for playing all drives. There is strength in a ball that flies on a similar curve to that on which the club circles the body; so there is always a bit of extra yardage to be found when a draw is played.

How?

By examining the sequence of how a hook shot may happen when not required, you will find the order in which adjustments must be made to apply hook. Great care must be taken, for only the gentlest introduction of these ingredients will cause quite a twist on the ball. When making a draw spin, a mere 'suggestion' should be enough.

Sequence

1. **Clubface** The merest turning-in of the clubface will impart a hook-spin to the ball. Care must be taken when turning in the straighter-faced clubs. The driver, with only 12 degrees of loft, does not have to turn inwards very far before it is deprived of sufficient loft to lift the ball.

2. **Hands** If the player adds to his vision the knuckles of the left hand, at the same time allowing the right hand to fall back, he will create a hooker's grip. This version of the grip is often favoured by people who have weak wrists, as a means of adding strength.

3. **Ball position** The ball should be brought back in the stance, for this allows the backswing to move further inwards for the in-to-out swing of the hook.

4. **Stance** A wider stance than normal is taken up. This causes more shoulder-turn, as though to make up for the lack of leg work.

5. **Line-Up** The right foot would be drawn back behind the left, appearing to aim off to the right of the target.

6. **Posture** The shoulders would be, like the feet, drawn into a line aiming away to the right and the left shoulder would appear higher than in normal shots.

7. **Backswing** The much stronger impression of arms-and-shoulders than of hand-and-wrist action in the backswing would create a spinning movement.

8. **Downswing** The important feeling is that the clubhead is journeying towards the ball from way behind the player in a scythe-like movement, and on a journey which would appear to be about to send the ball off towards the right of the target.

9. **Throughswing** From the in-to-out direction of the downswing, the hands manoeuvre the clubface *up* and *over* and cause the ball to start its out-to-in hook-spin.

As in all creative shots, mild application of the required ingredients is essential, particularly when only a slight draw is required. What actually happens in a hook, on the 'department-percentage' basis, is that there is a greater amount of turning from the arms-

and-shoulders 'department' than from that of the hands and wrists. The swing-path of the club from in-to-out encourages this; and the wide stance, stifling any chance of good footwork, adds to the need for shoulder-turn. The subsequent widened arc, created by the big shoulder movement, gives the power that makes hooks travel farther than slices.

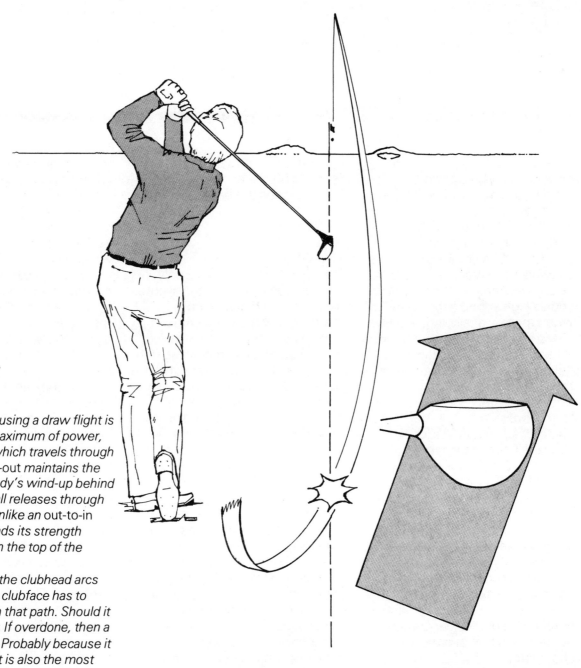

DRAW

The advantage of using a draw flight is that it gives the maximum of power, for a swing path which travels through the ball from in-to-out maintains the strength of the body's wind-up behind the ball so that it all releases through the hitting area; unlike an out-to-in swing which spends its strength coming away from the top of the backswing.

However, as the clubhead arcs from in-to-out the clubface has to close slightly from that path. Should it fail a push results: If overdone, then a hook can happen. Probably because it is the best flight, it is also the most difficult to attain.

PS Sandy Lyle, one of the game's longest hitters, favours this flight.

CHAPTER 31 — HIGH AND LOW SHOTS

Slice and hook shots are often played in windy conditions. A player should never fight strong winds but always send the ball off into the wind, with a flight that will benefit from having the wind behind it on its downward course. However, the types of shot to be discussed here are the two basic shots: *high shots,* to be played when there is a tailwind; and *low shots,* to be played when the wind is head-on. The instructions are deliberately few and are given in the sequence order.

High Shots

The ball is positioned slightly forward in the stance; even to the extent that the hands do not appear to be ahead of the shaft.

The stance would be narrowed slightly — otherwise, ground might be hit before the club reached the ball in its forward position.

In the backswing there would be an impression of more active hand-and-wrist action, with the percentage of this 'department' greater than that of arms and shoulders.

Altogether, there is a distinct feeling of 'flick' about the shot, which tosses the ball higher into the air and gives it all the benefits of a chasing wind.

Low Shots

Playing into wind is extremely difficult because even the slightest flaw, with its resulting spin, is magnified by the wind with often quite disastrous results. The less activity going on in the swing, the more solid the balance and thus the better the chance of control. To keep the ball as low as possible is quite an art, for the ingredients used tend to subtract so many degrees of loft from the face that the ball is often smothered.

The ball should be positioned back in the stance, which is widened to give a greater slant-back of the shaft from hands to clubhead.

During the swing there should be a mental bandaging of the wrist joints; the last thing required here is anything that will promote flick. The department working most, therefore, is that of the arms and shoulders and the ball is driven forward by a very solid movement where everything stays 'in one piece'.

To choose a less lofted club is good advice; not just because it is needed to make up for yardage which will be lost due to the wind, but because the player may take up his grip farther down the handle. A club held a couple of inches from the top helps keep wrists very still during the swing.

Though the high and the low shots have been given here with a view to their application in windy conditions, they may, of course, be applied also when an obstacle lies between ball and target.

When you need to get up and over a high tree, or even to land a ball on a green which has a bunker closely guarding the pin; this is an ideal time to add some of the high-shot skills.

Out and under the branches of a tree, or even when the player prefers to have his ball run up a bank guarding the green, rather than chance carrying right over the top, is ideal for the low shot.

Who says you must have a long backswing in order to send the ball a long way? Here Lee Trevino demonstrates the perfect control of his three-quarter length backswing as he prepares to launch a no. 3 wood shot on a very long journey.

(Bert Neale)

PART SIX — CLUB AND COMPETITIVE PLAY

CHAPTER 32 — FORMATS

In order to play golf in either match play (in which players take on opponents on a hole-by-hole basis) or in stroke play (in which a competitor's total score is matched against those of the other players), a handicap must be obtained. The object of this handicap is to allow the not-so-good player — by means of subtracting the allowed amount of strokes from the actual figure scored, on each hole in match play or from the total in stroke play — to be the equal of the good player. It is surprising just how well this system works, to the point of enabling the ordinary weekend player to enjoy

competing even against professionals.

To gain a handicap, it is essential to be a member of a Golf Society (although their handicaps are not always acceptable) or a member of a recognised Golf Club at which one plays regularly enough to be assessed for ability. This assessment system usually involves the completion of at least three rounds of golf in the company of a member of the Club, and the accurate recording of the scores taken for all three 18-hole games. This indicates to the Club's handicapping committee (or it may be the Secretary who decides) the

ability of the player. An average from the three score-cards determines how many strokes above the par of the course it takes the player to get round; and approximately that amount is granted in future rounds as the player's handicap. Normally, the highest allowance for men is 24 and for ladies and youngsters, 36.

As the player improves, his handicap allowance will be providing him with scores better than par, and the handicap will therefore be reduced. Unfortunately, there are some who prefer to retain, often for financial gain, a higher handicap than their ability would suggest. Such players are known as 'phoneys': a breed generally unwelcome in a game which enjoys an unparalleled reputation for sportsmanship. Others who, through vanity, cling to a low handicap to which they can never play spoil the pleasure of golf for themselves as well as for others by trying to achieve that which they cannot.

Often players find that they can play many of the 18 holes very well but, whether the reason is psychological or simply a weakness in the swing, they falter just once or twice. The high score taken when things go wrong tends to push up their handicap, with the result that they do very well in the match-play events and badly in those which are in the form of stroke play. There is, however, the opening for a handicap to be granted on general play, based on how well the good holes are played.

All in all, golf's handicapping arrangements are as fair as possible; after all, if it worked perfectly all tournaments would result in ties for first place! The experienced player views another's winning score in the light of reason: had he, the loser, played his best, he could have equalled the other's score. If the winner's score is many strokes beyond the experienced player's 'best', however, the winner may be suspected of being a 'phoney'.

What is Par?

A par figure, based entirely on yardage, is set at each hole and the total of the 18 holes gives the 'par for the course'.

Par 3 Any hole up to a yardage of 250 yards is deemed to be a par 3, on the principle that a good player can reach that distance in one stroke. There is, set into the par, an allowance of two putts to make up the total.

Part 4 Over 250 yards and up to 475 yards is within the reach of two strokes by a good player; so these, with the putting allowance, make up the par of 4.

Par 5 Over 475 yards is considered to be out of range of two strokes by the good player and holes beyond that yardage are par 5s.

In some parts of the world, there are holes which are out of reach in three strokes. These are set as Par 6s; but are so few and far between that there is no set yardage for them.

The United States measures vary slightly and are as follows Par 3 — up to 250 yards; Par 4 — from 250 yards to 470 yards; Par 5 — from 471 yards upwards.

In addition to the par settings there is, in many countries, what is known as a Standard Scratch Score (S.S.S.) for a course. This may be either more than the par total would suggest, or less. It is a system that gives a true picture of the difficulty of the course, for there may be a hole only a yard or so longer than a par 3 on one course, while another on a different course might be a yard less than a par 5; yet both are officially par 4s. S.S.S. may be reduced on the course that has several of the former, and increased on that which has some of the latter.

The system also allows for a downhill hole which, though its yardage may designate a par of 5, plays like a par 4; or an uphill par 3 hole that may simply be out of reach.

MATCH PLAY

Match play (which most golfers prefer, because the requirement of consistency is not such a premium as in stroke play) may be played as a *single*, in which two players oppose each other; as a *foursome*, in which two players, sharing a ball

by alternating hits, take on another pair doing the same; or in a *fourball* match, in which both players in a team match the score of their best ball against that of an opposing team.

The game is decided on a hole-by-hole result and the team recording the most wins is victorious. Should the sides be even after the round, then the match is 'all square'. If a result is required, however, further holes must be played on a 'sudden-death' basis. The method of subtracting handicaps in match play is: at the end of each hole, the team in receipt of a stroke (or strokes) subtracts it (or them) from the total taken at the hole and matches the net figure with that of the opposition. In an even match, a lower net figure would make the team 1-up; a higher net figure would make them 1-down. The match proceeds around the course until one team is more holes up than there are holes yet to play.

Unfortunately, the handicap system in match play is not straightforward, since different fractions of handicaps made are taken according to the type of match. The fractions for each type of match are as follows:

Single: The player with the highest handicap receives ¾ of the difference

Foursome: ³⁄₈ of the combined handicap of each team and the team with the highest total receives difference.

Fourball: ¾ of the difference between the handicap of the lowest player in the four and the other is taken.

In order that opponents know where handicap strokes are given, a stroke-index is marked on the scorecard of the course. Normally, the most difficult hole on the course is stroke 1, and the next most difficult, preferably on the other 'nine' (second half of the course), is stroke 2 and so on. Therefore, for example, a player in receipt of a 6-shot allowance would receive one stroke at all holes indexed as 6 and under.

STROKE PLAY

A stroke play round requires that all 18 holes be completed and the amount taken on each recorded in its appropriate space on the score-card. (Failure to do this accurately results in disqualification.) All 18 figures are added together and the total is the player's 'gross' score. From that is deducted the full handicap allowance to arrive at the net score.

However, the full handicap is not allowed when the competitor is part of a team. Here again, fractions are worked out which are considered fair to the type of event; depending on whether it is a *foursome* (score made by two players, playing alternate shots, sharing a ball) or a *better-ball*, in which the recorded score on each hole is the best of those taken up by either of the two players.

Stroke play Handicap Chart
Single: The full handicap
Foursome: ½ of the combined handicap
Fourball: The full handicaps

STABLEFORD COMPETITIONS

Another form of play is stableford golf, which owes popularity to its tolerance, which allows the player who takes a couple of disastrous holes to compete in 18-hole events where a total score counts. It also rewards a player who has done exceptionally well on a hole, over another who has done only quite well. At the same time, it doesn't punish the player who did reasonably well as harshly as it does one who fares badly.

The system is this: after deducting the allowed handicap as stated on the stroke index on the card, on completion of the hole, the player matches the net score against the par for the hole. Should he equal it, he receives 2 points. If he betters it by *one* stroke, he gets 3 points; and so on. If, on the other hand, only one stroke is dropped to par, then 1 point is gained; and more than one receives no points at all.

Like the other forms of golf, stableford may also be played as singles, foursomes, or fourball.

Stableford Chart
Single: 7/8th of the handicap
Foursome: 7/16th of the combined handicap
Fourball: 7/8ths of the handicaps

OTHER FORMS OF PLAY

While match play, stroke play, and stableford are three accepted forms of golf, there are many other versions. Some humorous, all enjoyable, they are unfortunately altogether too numerous to be mentioned more than briefly here.

Greensome foursomes, is popular after a good lunch, for it allows every player to hit a tee shot, yet is a brisk form of golf. The decision must be made by the team's two players, after the tee shot, as to which ball they will continue playing the hole with. From that moment, alternate strokes are played — the player whose ball is picked up commences by hitting that driven by his partner.

Another way of playing that has sprung up in recent years (often as forerunner to a major professional event where a sponsor's guests are being entertained) is a *Texas scramble.* This allows even the worst of hackers to experience playing from the positions encountered by a long-hitting pro.

As many as four or five players may participate, and all play the tee shots. The ball that finishes in the best position is chosen and all the other are retrieved and carried to that spot.

The players all play the next shot from that one place, and so they proceed up the hole. It is quite remarkable how often, during the round, the high-handicap player contributes, perhaps with a lucky iron-shot or by holing a long putt: there are no handicaps allowed here.

Many Golf Clubs issue a 'certificate of handicap', which may be shown by its members when visiting other clubs. Due to the ever-increasing numbers wishing to play golf, however, gaining membership is not always easy — many clubs have waiting lists which may take several years to climb. Golfers, and would-be golfers, who have no membership are obliged to play on the municipally owned courses, on privately owned pay-as-you-play courses, or simply to hit golf balls at driving ranges. There are many Clubs which, though they take limited numbers of green-fee payers, insist that the visitor produces a Handicap Certificate, as proof of his experience and ability, and as guarantee that he will not be likely to cause damage to the course or hold up play.

The correct procedure for a would-be member of a Club is to make an appointment to see the Secretary. The Secretary is a very important person: Club members expect him to protect their enjoyment of the course and the Club facilities by keeping off undesirable people. The attitude of firmness shown by Club Secretaries is often misinterpreted by inexperienced applicants, who cannot reconcile the apparent abruptness with what is, after all, a sport. However, the applicant himself will sooner or later appreciate the fact that the Club Secretary is merely striving to retain the tradition of golf. Without its traditions and codes of behaviour golf — both as a sport and as a way of life — might cease to be the envy of all other sports. Because golfers, no matter how high in the game they have climbed, are heavily penalised for even the slightest misdemeanour, the game has earned itself a sound reputation for fairness and therefore universal respect. It is good advice, therefore, to treat both the Club and its Secretary with respect on that opening visit.

Generally, the potential member is given an application form and required to obtain the 'backing' of two full members of the Club — who, when they sign the form, are taking on a degree of responsibility; indeed, almost guaranteeing the character of the applicant. It remains for the Club's committee (who have been voted into office by their fellow-members) to interview the applicant for approval. In some cases, a mid-week membership is offered until a space for full membership arises. Often, acceptance means only acceptance to a waiting list. One Glasgow Club sends its waiting members to a course they own many miles away on the coast; only after several years are they allowed 'to come in from the cold' to the senior club. This is a particularly fine Club, whose procedures are accepted without question — in exactly the same way that only formal dress is accepted in many clubhouses. Golf is none the worse for its disciplines.

Many of the public courses on which most novices begin playing (after all, it is natural to 'give it a try' before investing in membership fees or expensive equipment) have Clubs formed in association with the course. A small annual fee, additional to normal green fees, is often required; but the arrangement does allow players to compete against one another and, most important, to acquire that all-important handicap — an additional asset when filling in an application form to join another Club.

GOLFING MANNERS AND SAFETY

There is no more unwelcome creature on a busy golf course than the novice player; even worse, two novices playing together. Often their lack of experience leads them to be not only bad-mannered but quite dangerous. The expression which covers golfing manners and behaviour is *etiquette:* this provides the means whereby a player, even though he or she might not be playing too well, may allow others either in the group or on the course to enjoy their play.

The safety factor in golf must be clearly appreciated. Terrible injuries can be inflicted by both the swinging club and the flying ball. No player should ever attempt to play a ball until the golfers ahead are out of range, unless those players have 'waved' him through. (They would do this if they were holding up play — perhaps because a ball was lost; or because, as a four-ball, they were travelling more slowly than a singles match.) It is also wrong for anyone to play a stroke, or even to swing a

club in practice, until he has ascertained where his playing companions are standing. Carelessness at this point inflicts the serious injuries; the swinger's clubhead striking an unsuspecting partner, for instance. In many cases both are to blame, for it is the partner's duty to stand in the correct spot while the other plays. The place to be, particularly on the teeing area where the players are close together, is to the right of the tee, in full view of the striker but never ahead of the ball (for balls often fly off in the most unexpected directions).

It is etiquette to be still and silent while an opponent or partner plays his stroke, for the striking of a stationary ball requires more concentration than a moving one. While a soccer team may gain inspiration from thousands of screaming fans, a golfer certainly

does not; the merest blowing of a nose, the striking of a match or the rattling of a club coming out of a bag, can destroy what is often a very sensitive balance of concentration, particularly when the striker is not playing too well.

Consideration for the course is expected from all players and neglect in this area of golfing behaviour has no excuse. Any player who removes a divot from the course, be it fairway or rough, should retrieve it, replace it and tread it into place. The footprints made in bunkers, as well as the trough made by the striking club, should be smoothed out. When there is no rake handy, the back of the sand-iron and the sole of the shoe are capable of leaving a surface fair for those playing behind.

A ball pitching into the surface of a putting-green tends to drive a plug of turf under ground. This should be raised by means of a pitchfork, which may be obtained in the Club's professional's shop. Failure to bring the damaged area back to level will cause a permanent pit mark in the green.

Great care should be taken when close to the hole itself. The player who is asked to attend the flag while his partner is putting, should stand at arms' length to the side of the hole; not only does this allow his partner a clear view, it also stops the feet of a heavy person from denting the ground around the edge of the hole.

Removal of the ball from the hole should never be done with the clubhead, even when the hole is full of water; for this can damage that rim of earth between the top of the metal cup and the turf. The hole's edge can suffer, too, from a pin being carelessly replaced.

The pin may be laid on the green's surface while putting is in progress, but it should be placed

It is essential when repairing a pitch mark on a putting green to bring the turf, which has been punched under by the ball, to the top surface. Should the player simply tap the ground level then the turf which is trapped below will rot, leaving permanent damage to the green.

A very good principle for all club golfers is to repair two pitch marks on each green: his own and one more for some idle devil playing up ahead. In this way good putting surfaces may be maintained.

rather than flung down; and it should be out of line-of-vision of the opponent lest it cause distraction. Clubs, bags and trolleys should never be on the putting surface, but placed at the side of the green (at a point which reduces to a minimum the need to walk back and forth to retrieve them). Novices are inclines to make unnecessary journeys, which take up time and annoy the golfers player behind. Where a good player whose ball is just over the green will take both pitching club and putter, the beginner tends to take the pitching club only. He then has to come all the way back for the putter, so doing the journey twice.

Should any game lose pace, so that a completely empty hole exists ahead, then it has 'lost ground' and must call the match behind through: once this has been done, even though the cause of the delay might have been a lost ball which is suddenly found, the players behind must still be allowed to progress by 'playing through'.

CHAPTER 34 — PSYCHOLOGY AND PRESSURE

Because a round of golf takes several hours to complete, there is ample time for the player's mental state to have a great effect on his performance. Many higher-handicap golfers never produce a game, when card and pencil are involved, that in any way resembles their play when matched against a chum in a friendly game. The pressure of having to record a score that might prove embarrassing causes a tension capable not only of shattering a poor method but also reducing a very good swinger to so nervous a state that his true game doesn't materialise.

Mental pressure plays a great part in the game of golf and it affects people in different ways. Some react well to it: it puts an edge on their game, and they are likely to display a form seldom equalled in their friendly games. On the other hand — and this applies to the majority of golfers — many apparently good players simply 'seize up' the moment they have a card and pencil in their pocket.

Many of those who crumble in a stroke play event thrive on match play. The reason for this is the fear that the total (recorded for all to see) of a stroke play competition will prove that the player is not as

good as he supposed himself. It is a fear born of embarrassment, and this is a pity; for the golf he plays during a friendly game or in match play may be his true form. Relatively few people are able to maintain their best form when under pressure.

The level at which a person will become susceptible to pressure is impossible to measure, whether it be in golf, in business or simply in life itself. A tiny putt can reduce a man capable of huge straight drives down the narrowest of fairways, to a nervous wreck. This particular affliction is called a 'twitch'; it has been known for a player so afflicted to be led from the course quite unable to get the putter away from the ball. There have been great players who would deliberately play well short of a green within reach, in order that the next shot would require a long pitch rather than the little chip shot they dreaded, if they should miss the target first time.

There are many instances of very good players failing to become great players because one particular area of their game, though executed efficiently during hours of practice, would crumble the moment the pressure came on. What can be learned from this is

that *when confidence slips out — exaggerated pressure slips in!* The moment a player allows himself to believe he might mishit a shot, or miss a short putt, he ensures that he will!

This might suggest that there is no way to combat a mental incapacity to play under pressure; and further suggest it would be as well not to compete at all. Happily, that is not the case. Certain precautions can be taken which will allow the average golfer to escape some of those pressures and so score better, with the result that a more consistent game is played and the confidence level thereby raised, which combats pressure and allows further progress to be made.

THE SENSIBLE APPROACH

It is reassuring to learn that every golfer, whatever his level of competence, is subjected to pressure. So it is not surprising that the novice who is scoring well and on his way to a 'best' score that may gain him a handicap, might well crumple completely over the closing holes. Pressure tightens the muscles and the flowing width goes from his arc, which reduces the angle of degrees available on the clubface. That is why the clubs

'Oh, the agony of it all!' Ray Floyd of the United States.

(Ken Lewis)

that suffer most are those with the smallest amount of loft, i.e., the driver and the no. 3 wood; and nos. 2 and 3 irons.

There are two places in a round where the novice should stay away from slightly lofted clubs: at the beginning, when there is a combination of tension-under-pressure and tension-out-of-stiffness, and at the closing of what looks like being a good round, when the former begins to get hold of him. The policy to be adopted is definitely *there is safety in loft!* Rather than a driver with its 12 degree face, a no. 3 wood could be used from a tee-peg. Then, from the ground, the 3 wood should be rejected in favour of a 4 or 5 wood, which would provide a combination of greater loft and shorter handle and added comfort for the player. Using an iron, such as a 2 or 3 with their long handles and straight faces, is difficult even for a well-established golfer; so for the novice tension brought about by pressure, there can be little hope of success. Much better to choose a middle iron, even if it means playing a little short of the objective.

Because golf is played over a period of hours, and a stationary ball is hit, mental pressures that have no time to take effect in quick, reflex-movement games have plenty of opportunity to thrive in the mind of the golfer. And that is why golf has so many psychological traditions. Out of these, 'gamesmanship' was born — an aspect of the game that should be viewed rather with humour than with the aim of deliberate application against an opponent (unless, of course, he starts it!) A common 'gamesmanship' trick in match play is to concede several short putts then, when the opponent feels sure the next will be given, ask him to putt it. This particular 'gamesmanship' tactic is intended to put the opponent under pressure and so ensure that he will miss. Of course, if he holes it, one might regret having conceded the others!

Another tradition in match play golf is that 'being two up, with only *five* to play, never wins'. It is amazing how often that claim is made by the party who is two down, and how often the tactic works. The sudden loss of a couple of holes can see the leader crumple completely, just as if tradition has ordained it.

There are many more examples of the art of applying pressure on an opponent. While most are distasteful (and indeed may lead to ugly scenes on the course), the efficacy of such measures does go to prove the value of mental control in golf. The player is undoubtedly vulnerable in a game where there is so much time to think.

STRATEGY AND TACTICS
Match play and stroke play involve two entirely different attitudes as far as strategy and tactics are concerned. In match play, there are occasions where care must be thrown to the wind; in stroke play, this must never be done.

Match play
The state of the match determines the way in which holes may be played. For example, there is no need for a player who is several holes ahead to take any risks. He should disregard his opponent's strategy and attempt to play the course; perhaps choose to play up short of a stream or ditch, rather than attempt an uncertain carry; select a 3 wood, or even an iron, from the tee when a wild tee shot might risk going out of bounds; from a fairway bunker, take no risk with a long shot but play

conservatively out for a good position on the fairway; on the green, not 'charge' the hole in the hope of getting a long putt in but simply roll the ball up close to the hole for a safe two putts. Let the struggling opponent attempt all the do-or-die strokes — with his current low morale, there is little hope of their coming off.

On the other hand, being well down in a match does mean that often a risk must be taken. There can be no point in playing a second shot safely short of the green, when the winning opponent is safely on it in fewer shots. Care might have to be thrown to the wind when the opponent is *dormie* (that is, as many holes in the lead as there are holes left to play). A halved hole is no use — it must be a win or nothing, so carrying the stream might have to be attempted; that long putt might have to be 'charged' (that is to say, forceful), for there can be no point in leaving it short.

These examples are given for a match that is clearly going one way. In normal circumstances, in a close match, the common-sense shots which would be played in a stroke-play event would apply.

Stroke play
The first attitude a golfer must have before embarking on a stroke play round, in which every stroke is recorded, is *to think ahead, never give up, and attempt to finish the round one shot better than might have been!* This attitude might just reward the player by ensuring a cool head at a moment when panic could easily set in. Thinking of the most sensible way out of a difficult situation, even though it means accepting what appears to be second best, more often than not turns out for the best. There are many rounds of golf completed where the player, in hindsight,

wishes he had settled for a bit of common-sense and not attempted the miracle shot which ended in tragedy.

The greatest mistakes made in golf are those that follow a mistake. Every golfer has mishits that visit the trees, the rough and the hazards; but the experienced good player accepts these and plays a sensible recovery stroke into a position from which he can do well with his next shot. He knows that a shot hit in anger, after the frustration of the first mishit, will succeed only in getting him into worse trouble.

When a tee shot is hit into the wrong position, leaving the flag positioned tightly behind deep bunkers, the player should play not directly at the flag but wide of it, into the largest area of green.

In thick rough, a straight-faced club will gather a lot of grass between blade and ball, with little hope of a clean hit. The selection of a lofted club, even though this may not be capable of reaching the green, will ensure a cleaner contact and therefore greater distance than a longer club.

When a player doubts that his best shot will carry a guarding hazard, such as a stream, he should not attempt it. The pressure alone will subtract from his natural length and the ball will not carry. Far better to lay up short and — who knows? — the result might be a pitch and single putt, with a par as the reward for clear thinking.

On the green, great consideration should be given not only to the long putt in hand but also to the one remaining if the first one should miss. Should the hole bu cut on a sloping part of the green, it is better that the ball arrives below rather than above the hole: after all, an uphill second putt may be hit firmly whereas a curly downhiller may lead to three putts being taken.

The hole should never be attacked when greens are very fast; it is better to allow for a greater borrow and attempt to drop the ball into the cup on its dying roll. There is nothing which breaks the spirit of a player quite like regular three-putting; for he is aware that poor players on the course, hitting hardly a single good shot, are scoring as well as he is — while all his own good play is being cancelled out over that last few inches to the hole.

Isao Aoki of Japan with his unique 'toe-up' putting action which, though often criticised, earned him more money than any other player in the World in 1978.

(Ken Lewis)

CHAPTER 35 — COURSES AND WEATHER

Different climates produce a great range of grasses and these, in turn, require a particular type of golf to be played. As a matter of fact, it was the thick American grass which necessitated production of the larger 1.68″ ball, for the 1.62″ British size, which was used at first in the States, simply sank too low for clean shots to be played.

It is not necessary to travel to the lush courses of the Far East, to the grain-grasses of South Africa, or to the wiry turf of North America in order to find contrasts. Within the British Isles there are many choices of turf. Around the coast there are the sand-based links courses, where the growth is tight to the ground. There are heathland courses, with short grass and springy turf. Parkland courses, which make up the majority, are inclined to be heavy and soggy when wet; but after a few days of sun in the summer, they soon become quite hard and bouncy.

It is a compliment to the skill of the game's professionals that they are able to adapt their game, virtually overnight, to suit these changes in condition by switching to the correct type of stroke. With as little as one practice round, even the youngest of American players switches from pitching the ball high in the air with lots of backspin, to producing chip-and-run shots worthy of a veteran Scot who has spent his life on links courses.

Links Turf

Links turf is on a base of sand and is so windswept that the growth is very limited. The difficulty is to get the bottom edge of the club below the ball without hitting the ground first; the old Scottish word 'sclaff' originated from this common mishit. The best way to play on links turf is to use only wooden clubs with the shallowest faces, such as nos. 4 and 5. Then the ball may be brought back to a more central position in the stance (an action which delofts the face) so that the ball may be caught before the club has a chance to hit the ground. Hitting the ground first on links has an effect very different from doing the same thing on inland courses; on links, the club will bounce rather than penetrate, and many shots will be topped.

There has to be increased hand action with iron shots, for they often have to be punched from a tight lie. Once again, the ball may be brought back in the stance and a more lofted club used. It must be stressed that the use of a lofted club is not defeatist and there is no intention of playing deliberately short of the green. You will recall, from the chapter on 'shaping-shots', that a ball brought back in the stance encourages a hook spin, which causes the ball to run and so travel farther. What must not be expected from such a swing is backspin; but links are in any case not designed for stop shots.

The greens on links courses are very undulating and extremely fast-running, so it would be folly to attempt pitching balls up to the flag. Bouncing in, with chip-and-run shots, from short of the green is the correct procedure — and the ability to judge the effect of the bounce is most important. Many shots have to be played away from the flag towards a safe area of the green, when a deep bunker lies between it and the player; and that really sums up links golf. It is the player who can position each shot so that the pin becomes approachable from the correct direction with his next, who does best.

Inland Courses

Inland courses are much easier to play. Their softer fairways 'sit the ball up', making it simpler to hit. The soft receptive greens, which hold a good shot within inches of its first bounce, allow the player to 'come in' from many angles which, on a links, would be impossible. Golf in these circumstances becomes much more straightforward, and adaptability thus carries a lower premium. Nevertheless, there are certain guide lines which should be adhered to.

Tee-shots are the most important shots and they must be kept 'in play'. Having to play sideways from a forest or out of bushes is very expensive, so the player must carefully determine, before driving, the best side of the hole to play the second shot from; and then make every effort to drive down that side. Often, using the driver should be avoided in favour of a more lofted wood, especially when trouble lies to the right. Loft keeps control on the ball because of the strength of its extra backspin, and reduces the chance of a slicing flight.

Playing recovery shots over very high trees should be avoided in favour of a sensible shot played wide, even though that may appear cowardly; for a deflection off that 'last little twig right at the very top' can prove disastrous.

The pitching-wedge must become the favourite club, and should be much used in practice; for it is *the* most important stroke-saving weapon. The knowledge that the greens are holding permits

The texture of the soil on the seaside links can still offer problems to the professionals. Ken Brown punches his ball from a tight sandy trough.

(Ken Lewis)

the player to hit confidently up to the pin, and so to save a stroke where one might easily be dropped.

It is much easier to assess how a putt will perform on inland courses than it is on links. Inland, the grass tends to grow more quickly and is therefore cut more often. The best way to read a green for nap is to look for the 'shine' as opposed to the 'dull', just as one looks at a lawn which has just been mown. One strip is light in colour and the next is dark yet, from the other end of the lawn, those strips would appear to be the opposite. This is because light shows the blades leaning *away* from the onlooker to be shining, and those leaning *towards* him, so casting a shadow, to be dark. So, when lining up a putt, if the green is seen as shining, the ball will be aided by an easy roll and will travel well, even from a gentle strike; yet, coming from the other side, which will be into dull grass, it will require a firm hit.

Bunkers vary greatly, from the light white sand on seaside courses and the odd sandy-soiled inland course, to what can only be described as the raked-up brown earthy substance of the clay-based courses.

The players seen splashing balls from bunkers on your television screen are usually sufficiently privileged to be playing either on links or at a top inland course that has provided the very expensive light sand. Even they would have to resort to aiming further behind the ball and hitting harder, with little hope of backspin, were they to play from some of the heavy inland sand bunkers.

WEATHER
The determination of golfers to play regardless of weather has taught us how to adapt to foul conditions — even how to turn them, wherever possible, to advantage. Unless greens are flooded or buried in snow, or there is lightning about, golf goes on and the best must be made of existing conditions.

Rain
In persistent rain, club handles become slippery and gloves soggy, so scores are going to be higher for everyone. Being sensible enough to accept this fact is important. Ideas of attempting any risky shots should be dismissed from the mind; instead, more sensible positional shots should be attempted.

In thick rough, which is doubly difficult when soaking wet, no attempt should be made to cover long distances. The player should be content with hitting the ball, using a very lofted iron, back to the fairway.

On the fairway, straight-faced clubs are difficult because the wet blade tends to skid the ball. Much better contact is made by choosing a more lofted club and the same applies on tee shots, where a 3 wood is safer.

Pitching to the green should be done with the more lofted clubs only, since assessing the distance the ball will travel across the wet surface, should a chip-and-run shot be played, is almost impossible. Besides, the wet green will provide even more stop on to a lofted approach.

When putting, allow for a much reduced amount of borrow, for the added weight of the hit required to get the ball to the hole on a wet green will keep the ball on a straighter course. In fact, all putts from a distance of four feet or closer may, unless the player is on an exceptional slope, be hit straight at the hole.

Wind
The good striker of the ball is the one who usually does best in strong windy conditions, for a well-balanced swing will obviously withstand the buffeting. However, there are many ways in which even an average player can use the wind as an aid rather than be defeated by it; for wind creates a 'swings and roundabouts' situation, in which what might be lost 'going against it' could be gained when 'going with it'. Nevertheless, it must be remembered that it is the same for everyone else on the course and scoring is bound to be higher all round.

Into *headwind,* a loss of distance will be inevitable and it is pointless to attempt to hit harder as a means of making up the loss. The extra activity of the hand-and-wrist action when such an attempt is made simply exaggerates the amount of backspin imparted to the ball, so it in fact goes even less distance. Instead, the player should attempt to swing as smoothly as possible, keeping the wristwork to a minimum, then the ball, with a minimum of backspin, will move through the wind and travel far enough.

In fierce headwinds, all approach shots should be played with a straight-faced club, rather like large chip-and-run shots. When the loft of a wedge backspins the ball, all control is lost. When the approach is from only a short distance and there is a bunker in the way, the wind becomes an asset, for the ball can be tossed right at the flag. The fear of going into the sand is eliminated by the certain knowledge that the wind will stop the ball from overshooting.

There is even comfort in hitting a putt into the wind; for the knowledge that the roll will cease abruptly encourages the player to attack the hole.

Downwind has obvious advantages. Not only will it carry

the ball further, it will also buffet the curves out of the flight and so keep it on a straighter course. Thus, the player will get much closer to the green from tee shots, even bringing par 5 holes within reach of two shots, and long par 4s within pitching-club range.

From the fairway, more will be gained if extra height is achieved; so a no. 5 wood (which is much easier to use, anyway) will travel as far as the more difficult no. 3 wood. The same applies to the irons: the easier no. 5 will cover distances that would normally require a no. 3 iron.

The disadvantage of travelling downwind is that there might be no backspin to help stop the ball on landing; most of it will have been blown out. It is therefore necessary to allow for 'run after landing', though this might require the ball's first bounce to be short of the green. What does one do when a bunker lies in the path? One plays up safely wide of the bunker and settles for a longer putt.

Crosswinds are very difficult, though the one that blows at the player's chest at line-up is easier than that which blows at his back. The former tends to push him back on his heels, which shallows the arc: a shallow arc is a powerful way of swinging and good distance is gained with such a wind. The wind from the back tips the player onto his toes and steepens the arc: an upright arc is the weakest version, in which the ball will be sliced into a short, vulnerable flight.

The wisdom of the good player lies in his acceptance of these statistics. He allows for them by starting the ball's journey off into the wind: then it is allowed to travel the rest of its journey with the strength of the wind behind it. It is a foolish player who attempts to fight wind — and an even more foolish one who believes that the wind won't affect the ball.

CHAPTER 36 — RULES

Although most of the great golfing nations set their own rules of golf, they are based on those set by the Royal and Ancient Golf Club at St. Andrews, traditional home of the game. The United States Golf Association works hand-in-glove with the R & A to see that as few conflicting rules as possible exist.

Booklets on rules are published and each golf-club Secretary is in possession of one; thus he is often called upon to adjudicate in a query or dispute. The occasional apparently insoluble problem that arises is sent to St. Andrews for a ruling; and that ruling is binding.

As one might imagine, hitting a ball over several miles of countryside can result in all sorts of problems and the Rules of Golf aim to provide for all of them. It is therefore pointless to attempt to cover them in this book; much better that the reader obtains his own copy and keeps it, safe and dry, in the pocket of his golf bag.

'With a bit of luck that could finish close . . .'

'. . . it might even go in . . .'

'. . . it is going in!'

'How could it miss? . .'

'*****!!!' Sandy Lyle with the one that got away.

(Ken Lewis)

PART SEVEN — AN AFTERWORD ON PROFESSIONALISM

There are two clearly defined branches of professional golf. In the first, a player matches his (or her) ability against that of other professionals in competition for prize money. In the other, a professional sets up in business and is retained by a Golf Club, where he makes his livelihood by his ability to teach the game and by supplying the required equipment to his members.

CHAPTER 37 — THE TOURNAMENT PROFESSIONAL

In order to convert from amateur golfer to tournament professional, it is essential to join the Tournament Players' Division of the Professional Golfers' Association (PGA). To do that, the player must be able to satisfy the following requirements:
1. He must be of a handicap of 1 or better.
2. He must attend a PGA school for potential tournament players and compete against other applicants, over four rounds, to win a Player's Card. These schools, normally held annually, take not only new applicants but also those players who did not finish in the set number of top places the previous year. (In Europe, it would be those below the top 150 who would have to re-apply.) The field of applicants can be very large and only a small percentage will qualify to enter tournaments as Card holders.

Being a Card holder does not automatically ensure an easy income. Once the circuit begins, every player has to pay a high entrance fee for each event. Even that only gets him into the pre-qualifying round — not into the tournament proper. If he fails to get a place for the final stages (and he has to get into the top 60 to win a place), he moves on to the next venue for the following pre-qualifying round.

It is a hard and expensive road with no guarantee of success; and many who try without the aid of sponsorship simply fall by the wayside.

On a more optimistic note: the applicant who does become a money-winner gains not only a very fruitful living but also enjoyment of all the advantages of travel and the competitive lifestyle.

The lady professionals in the great golfing nation of the USA operate a school exactly like the men; but, then, there are so many more women players in the States. In Europe, there is not yet the demand for a qualifying school for ladies; though no doubt it will come before very long.

Where many lady golfers are found to be up on the toes of the left foot at the moment of impact here we see the opposite. Donna Caponi Young, a top United States Lady Professional, who is a very solid striker of the ball is solidly on her left heel.

(Ken Lewis)

CHAPTER 38 — THE CLUB PROFESSIONAL

Although the standard of play required of an apprentice golf professional is not as high as that required of the tournament player, it is still very demanding. The apprentice must be of single-figure handicap, and during his registration must complete three competitive rounds in PGA event of not more than 4 over the scratch score of the course. Failure to do so requires him to test his playing ability in a qualifying event, before being allowed to sit his end-of-registration examinations. Successful completion of three rounds of such scoring during his three-year registration eliminate the requirement to prove his ability and allow him to sit the final examinations during his third year.

These final examinations test his ability to run a golf shop that would provide a satisfactory service to Club members. He must have a sound knowledge of the golf swing and be able to teach to the satisfaction of the examining board.

He must be capable of completing all types of repairs on a bench, so that a minimum of cost and delay would be incurred by customers. His capacity for accurate book-keeping and accounting, other important factors in the successful running of a Club shop, is also tested.

His appreareance is under scrutiny and his knowledge of the Rules of Golf is tested. These are both very important facets of the Club professional. (In Great Britain, the enthusiasm for encouraging high professional standards has led the Royal and Ancient Committee to donate large sums of money annually to improve the all-round training of apprentice professionals.)

Once successfully through his finals, he may apply to golf clubs advertising for a professional. He will be interviewed along with others who get on the short list of applicants; and, if successful, will thereafter be responsible for stocking a shop which will provide satisfactorily for the Club members. In time, the new professional will take on his own junior, who will both assist and be trained by him.

The responsibility of the Club is to provide a suitable facility from which the new professional may operate. The Club also pays a retaining fee, which is determined by the size of the membership and the Club's financial position. Members are then expected to support the Club professional; and by so doing, they enable him to provide a service which can make their own golf more enjoyable.

AUG. 1982. 3-D. GOLF WEEK: MEON VALLEY DAI REES & JOHN GARNER

" 2ND (J.G.) GRIP (OK) SET-UP. (i) CHECK GRIP; BOTTOM EDGE TO TARGET. HANDS TO LEFT
   KNEE WITH LEGS TOGETHER: STANCE RELATED TO FOOT WIDTHS

3RD (JG/DR) SWING TRACK. FROM 4 O'CLOCK to 10 O'CLOCK - OUT TO IN - TURN LEFT
SHOULDER TAKING CLUB INSIDE LEFT KNEE TRACKS TOWARDS RIGHT KNEE (NOT
TOWARDS BALL) DOWNSWING TRACK DOWN WITH ARMS AND HANDS TRACKING
OUTWARDS OF LINE TO TARGET, KEEP THE LEFT SHOULDER HIGH (RIGHT
SHOULDER LOW UNDERNEATH FEELING OR CROSSING)
TWO EXERCISES. (a) TAKE CLUB BACK ON 4 O'CLOCK TRACK WITH LEFT HAND
& SHOULDER RETURNING THRO THE 'HIT' TO 10 O'CLOCK KEEP SHOULDERS
ON LINE, RIGHT SHOULDER DOWN (b) SWING RIGHT ARM UNDER OUTSTRETCHED
LEFT ARM TO ENCOURAGE RIGHT SHOULDER TO GO LOW UNDER LEFT
ARM

5TH PITCH (JG) HANDS FORWARD, WEIGHT ON HEELS, CLOSENESS ESSENTIAL
SLOW BACK, FIRMLY FORWARD SQUEEZING THE BALL
   PUTTING (JG) REVERSE O'LAP LEFT ELBOW ON LINE, FACE THE BALL TO A
3 FOOT CIRCLE AT THE HOLE
   BUNKERS (i) NORMAL   OPEN STANCE, WEIGHT ON LEFT FOOT. OPEN THE FACE
CHECK GRIP, STEEP BACK SWING, SLOWLY, FIRMLY FORWARD RIGHT
THROUGH TO FLAG, COVER GREEN WITH SAND. CHECK THE OPEN FACE
LONGER SHOTS HARDER HIT USE THE RIGHT KNEE THRO THE LINE
(ii) PLUGGED, SQUARE STANCE, CLOSED FACE CHOP DOWN AFTER SLOW BACK
(LIFT) SWING, KEEP THE CLUB GOING THRO' AS BEFORE. BALL SQUIRTS OUT.
(iii) UP-FACE SQUARE STANCE, NOT AN OPEN FACE, GO ALONG THE LINE OF
THE BUNKER DON'T FALL BACK. KEEP GOING THRO TO FLAG
ESSENTIAL USE OF RIGHT HAND ON DOWN SWING TO THROW THE
BALL ALONG THE LINE OF TARGET. (DR)
   IRON PLAY (REVISION) TAKE AWAY, TURN LEFT SHOULDER, LIFT SQUARE
WITH TRIGGER RIGHT HAND SLOW BACK FIRMLY THRO TO TEN
ROUTINE FOR PRACTICE 2 SWINGS WITHOUT BALL CHECKING, (i) SQUARE TO
TARGET ALONG SWING PLANE
6TH REVISION KEEP THE RIGHT SHOULDER BACK ON LINE THROW LEFT SHOULDER
HIGH AND FORWARD LEFT ARM FORWARD OF BENT RIGHT ARM
   DRIVER HIGH TEE SLOW BACK SHOULDER, HANDS & ARMS THRO TO 10 O'CLOCK